Methuen Playscripts

The Methuen Playscripts series exists to extend the range of plays in print
by publishing work which is not yet widely known but which has already
earned a place in the repertoire of the modern theatre.

Close the Coalhouse Door

One of the striking features of Britain in the late sixties has been the
resurgence of the theatre outside London. Audiences in Exeter, Stoke-on-
Trent, Liverpool, Manchester, Glasgow, Nottingham, Coventry and many
other places are being offered more and more premières of new work and,
in particular, of plays and shows written about the area where they are to
be staged.

Close the Coalhouse Door, written for the Newcastle Playhouse, where it
played for a total of nine weeks in 1968 and 1969, is one of the outstanding
'documentary' musicals to emerge in the regional theatre in recent years.
Its aims are simple: 'A hymn of unqualified praise to the miners — a group
of men who forged a revolutionary weapon without having a revolutionary
intent.'

'The terrible thing about history, said Orwell, is how few names of its slaves
have been preserved. Tenderly and furiously *Close the Coalhouse Door* does
a little to redress that injustice.'

Ronald Bryden in *The Observer*

CLOSE THE COALHOUSE DOOR

ALAN PLATER

First published in paperback 1969
by Methuen & Co Ltd
Reprinted 1971
First published in hardback 1971
Reprinted 1974 and 1976 by Eyre Methuen
11 New Fetter Lane, London EC4P 4EE

Copyright © 1969 and 1972 Alan Plater
Lyrics and tunes © 1969 and 1972 Alex Glasgow

Set by Expression Typesetters
Printed in Great Britain by
Fletcher & Son Ltd, Norwich

ISBN 0 413 29910 4

To the pitmen of Tyne and Wear
– to miners everywhere

Introduction

When *Close the Coalhouse Door* was running in Newcastle, it is recorded history that strong men, only able to obtain tickets for the Saturday matinée, voluntarily missed football matches to see the show: in the North East, greater love hath no man. This response, among the folk for whom it was created, was hardly anticipated when Bill Hays, a theatre and television director born in Wingate, Co. Durham, first suggested to the Newcastle Playhouse the idea of a show based on the history of the area.

Pitman-turned-novelist Sid Chaplin lives round the back of the Playhouse, though more elegantly than the phrase suggests, and the structure of the show was planned in Sid's front room at a four-way meeting involving the owner-occupier, Bill Hays, Alex Glasgow (a Gateshead singer and songwriter, son of a miner) and myself, a native of Jarrow, and no need to elaborate on that.

The intention was quickly established. A golden wedding party of an old pitman and his wife would form a springboard into reminiscence and reflection about the past: the personal and working dilemma of grandson John would push us into the future with, Sid's phrase, 'sibling jealousy to spice the plot.' It is impossible and irrelevant to divide the creative credit. I wrote the script from this collective notion, with the aid of a shelf-load of un-Establishment history books: the complete works of Chaplin ('The Thin Seam', published by Pergamon, contains the best short stories on mining since D. H. Lawrence): the title and title song, written a few months previously for a radio programme: the assurance that the BBC was backing the show: a PhD thesis on the General Strike obtained via a neighbour in Hull; and a hundredweight of inherited prejudice.

The historical material fell conveniently into a three-act pattern. The nineteenth-century oppression was the obvious Beginning: the between-the-wars chaos the inevitable Middle: and the post-Nationalisation non-Utopia the ambivalent End. In academic terms Proposition, Exposition and Resolution; in more appropriate music-hall terms, Information, Feed and Tag.

The evidence of Joan Littlewood's work at Stratford and Peter Cheeseman's at Stoke is that the ideal way of creating a free-wheeling musical based on community experience is to work with a long-established resident company, using collective improvisation as the main tool. In our case it was necessary to recruit a special company of those rare actors who talk, with utter conviction, in the accent of the North East; in practice this meant natives, with one or two talented exceptions. The text had to be precise but flexible, because a three-week rehearsal period leaves little room for changes of mind and indecision.

The show has grown and developed since the first night and there is no definitive script — nor should there be, for this or any play. This printed text corresponds to what happened on the stage of Nottingham Playhouse in October 1968, immediately before the London opening. Despite the episodic structure, the acts are shown as continuous: the pace and fluidity of the production proved that it is perfectly easy for an actor to switch, line by line, from being Lloyd George to himself and back to Lloyd George again, giving talent and conviction. A top-hat helps but is strictly optional.

I have included the same stage directions as in the first draft script. These are concerned with clarifying the dramatic intention in each sequence, which is more important than specifying whether Charles makes his exit behind or in front of the chaise-longue.

Half the songs were written specially for the show and the rest — including the title song — were from Alex Glasgow's extensive collected works. Contrary to some speculation, they are not based on traditional ballads, nor are they 'folk songs'. They are out of the composer's own head, drawing their inspiration from a long tradition of Tyneside music-hall songs.

The music-hall element is very important. One of the pleasant side-effects was that I was asked by a journalist whether I had been influenced by Brecht: and was able to reply, with total honesty, not so much Brecht as Jimmy James, Norman Evans, Dave Morris and Harry Mooney.

It is an actors' show, and forces them to use unfamiliar muscles: they must dance and sing, play a multitude of parts within an overall persona, and generally extend their technique beyond the normal demands of a talking-play. They must be free but not sloppy, flexible but not self-indulgent, constantly inventive but aware of an overall discipline. Just as the actors extend their range of expression, so the audience extends its range of perception, and it is clear that both welcomed the chance.

Shows based on community experience — a deliberate device to avoid the phrase 'documentary drama' — are proving to be great audience-winners in the new regional theatre. It is good to see full houses prepared to look, eye to eye, at theatre which reflects, and does not evade, their own experience. But there is a danger of introspection and parochialism and while most of these shows are many times more adventurous and gutsy than much West End fodder it may be that the next job is to use this collective experience without being seen using it. The hard look must not become the soft option.

Finally, of course, there is no such thing as cold objectivity, in theatre or anywhere else. We set off with inbuilt attitudes towards the subject and the stated aim of creating 'an unqualified hymn of praise to the miners, who created a revolutionary weapon without having revolutionary intention.' We selected those areas of history which confirmed our attitudes — though, as it happens, there were plenty to choose from. We were delighted that, in the process, it was possible to celebrate genuine heroic figures like Thomas Hepburn, and to correct the handy, economy-sized, child's encyclopaedia notion that the lot of the pitmen was improved simply by Lord Shaftesbury waving a magic wand.

Our subject has the final word. After the first night in Newcastle, I talked to a pitman, thirty years a Union man. 'Did we get it right?' I asked him. 'Yes,' he said, 'you got it right.'

Alan Plater
11 March 1969

Close the Coalhouse Door was first presented at the Newcastle Playhouse on 9 April 1968 with the following cast:

WILL JOBLING	Kevin Stoney
THOMAS MILBURN	Colin Douglas
EXPERT	Dudley Foster
MARY ANN MILBURN	Brenda Peters
VICAR	Robin Parkinson
JACKIE	John Woodvine
GEORDIE	Bryan Pringle
JOHN MILBURN	Alan Browning
FRANK MILBURN	Ralph Watson
RUTH	Geraldine Moffatt
SINGING PITWOMAN	Jean Becke
OTHER GUESTS	Catherine Brandon
	James Garbutt
	Fred Pearson
	Colin Hale
	Elayne Sharling
	Helen Stephenson
MUSICIANS	Bill Southgate (Musical Director)
	Jerry Rochefort (Drums)
	and members of the Craghead Colliery Band

Musical Direction by Bill Southgate
Setting and Lighting designed by Brian Currah
Directed by Bill Hays

The Newcastle production transferred to the Nottingham Playhouse on 7 October 1968 and to the Fortune Theatre, London on 22 October 1968.

Character Notes

THOMAS MILBURN: The same age as the century or thereabouts. An ex face worker. Talkative and cantankerous, and an aristocrat among working men.

MARY ANNE MILBURN: Thomas's wife, gently persuasive, with a manner toughened by years of hardship and sometimes violent bereavement. A life dedicated without question to her husband and, by implication, to coal.

JOHN MILBURN: The grandson who stayed home. In his early 30's, he is a skilled maintenance man and — away from the mine — likes food, beer, women, gambling and not too many questions.

FRANK MILBURN: The grandson who escaped, via education. In his mid-twenties, he is doing post-graduate research at Newcastle. Has a deep sense of the village's history with all the passionate outrage — and impotence — of the liberal academic.

RUTH: Frank's girl. The same age or a little younger. Not from the North-East — though not South Ken either — she is academic but not dozy with it. Uses dreaming spires as a vantage point, not a cell.

WILL JOBLING: Thomas's mate — same age and background — he complements the old man. They are bound by years of shared danger, and a common hatred of the bosses.

JACKIE: Sturdy, straight-thinking Union man. He knows the ropes and his history, and if he is played for caricature, the theare will be burned down.

GEORDIE: Jackie's mate, the local comedian, though all his jokes are edged with grey — or at least the awareness of grey. Jackie is a more or less conscious 'feed'.

THE VICAR: A more or less straightforward guy in his 30's — he'd have to have some kind of social awareness to accept the parish — and even if he didn't, he'd soon get it.

THE EXPERT: A kind of all-purpose Voice of the Fluctuating Them, he is a theatrical device rather than a character — but if he can develop a consistent persona in his various guises — and perhaps a kind of helplessness in the hands of a larger Destiny — that wouldn't be bad at all.

Thomas, Mary, John, Will, Jackie and Geordie *must* have convincing Geordie accents.

The Set

There are three main elements in the set.

First is the Milburn's cottage — for our purposes the single room in which the party is held. Very simply furnished, warm and cosy in the best sense of the word. I have assumed the house to be at one side of the stage — left or right — and occupying roughly half the stage area.

The other side of the stage, and probably further back, is the pithead, which obviously must be a kind of compromise between reality and what we can physically achieve on a stage. The essential elements are the cage — which need not move, providing we can create the illusion of movement — and, for purely visual/symbolic reasons — the pitwheel. The pithead must loom over the play in every sense.

Finally, a general outdoor area — outside the cottage and the pithead. This is simply empty stage which we fill as and when the need arises, which is plenty.

In general terms, it will be an asset to have some change of level in the set. The cottage could be slightly raised, and the entry to the cage could be higher still — from a kind of gantry.

I have assumed projection equipment and a screen, and briefly indicated the kind of things we can show, without filling out details. If this turns out to be impracticable, no matter: the essential items — dates and names — we write on placards and hang them on a nail.

Overall, the set should be simple and uncluttered. We want nothing that cannot be used.

ACT ONE

Darkness. The song begins and as it continues the lights go up to show the pithead and the slag-heap behind, grey but not without poetry. A solo voice, off-stage.

SONG:
    Close the coalhouse door, lad,
    There's blood inside.
    Blood from broken hands and feet
    Blood from hearts that know no beat
    Close the coalhouse door, lad,
    There's blood inside.

    Close the coalhouse door, lad,
    There's bones inside.
    Mangled, splintered piles of bones
    Buried 'neath a mile of stones
    And not a soul to hear the groans
    Close the coalhouse door, lad,
    There's bones inside.

    Close the coalhouse door, lad,
    There's bairns inside.
    Bairns that had no time to hide
    Bairns that saw the blackness slide
    Bairns beneath the mountainside
    Close the coalhouse door, lad,
    There's bairns inside.

    Close the coalhouse door, lad,
    And stay outside.
    Geordie's standin' at the dole
    And Mrs Jackson like a fool
    Complains about the price of coal
    Close the coalhouse door, lad,
    There's blood inside,
    There's bones inside,
    There's bairns inside,
    So stay outside.

(The song ends. A moment's silence then an electric bell rings, harshly. WILL JOBLING walks into a pool of light near the pithead.)

WILL: Divven' fret, Tommy lad, I can hear ye.

(WILL sets the winding gear in motion and the cage comes up to the surface – indicated by the noise of the machinery and lights fading up on the cage, with THOMAS MILBURN inside. He opens the gate and steps out.)

WILL: Are you all right, Tommy?

THOMAS: Aye, I'm all right.

WILL: Like it's the big day today, isn't it?

THOMAS: Aye, it's the big day all right.

(The EXPERT walks into a spotlight at the opposite side of the stage.)

EXPERT: Just one moment, please

(The OLD MEN pause.)

You're probably wondering who these men are and what they are doing. Well, briefly, this is a disused coalmine in the village of Broken-back . . . (Long 'o'.)

THOMAS: Brockenback. (Sharply, with short 'o'.)

EXPERT: Brockenback. (A good try.) However, this mine is linked by underground workings to the large, modern coalmine at Datton, five miles away. It is necessary to keep this shaft at . . . Brockenback open simply to keep the pumps in operation so as to avoid the danger of flooding at Datton. The pumping machinery is in the charge of these two gentlemen, working alternate shifts.

(Pause.)

Right. From the top of the cage, I mean the top of the page.

(WILL and THOMAS resume their conversation.)

THOMAS: What's it to be? Double or quits or a fresh game?

WILL: Double or quits.

THOMAS: Serves you right.

(THOMAS tosses two pennies in the air. They look eagerly to see how they fall. Obviously an old ritual.)

Two tails.

WILL: Ye bugger!

(WILL pays up.)

EXPERT: What you have just seen is an old miners' traditional pastime known as pitch and toss. Please regard me as your friend, ladies and gentlemen . . . available throughout the evening to explain these points, sort out problems of translation and . . .

THOMAS (sharply): Oh, hadaway to Hell!

(A brief reaction from the EXPERT — more hurt than angry — then he exits. Kill spotlight.)

Anyhow, you'll pop in the party later on . . .

WILL: Aye, I'll give the pumps a couple of hours on their own . . .

THOMAS: Just ring when you fancy it . . .

WILL: Oh, I'll not miss your party, Tommy. I mean, it's not every day you have a golden wedding, is it?

(WILL steps into the cage. THOMAS sets off the winding gear. We hear the machinery and the cage is lost in the darkness.)

THOMAS: Aye. It's not every day.

(Lights out on THOMAS and quickly up on the party in the house — lively but not raucous. Those present: MARY ANNE MILBURN, the VICAR, JACKIE, GEORDIE, PITMEN and their WIVES.)

VICAR: Where's the blushing bridegroom, Mrs Milburn?

MARY: Oh, he's out the back washing hisself . . .

VICAR: Cleanliness is next to Godliness, you know . . .

MARY: Aye, I never could see that, myself . . .

(GEORDIE steps forward.)

GEORDIE: Cleanliness, you say? You ought to meet wor lass. Oh, she's a disgusting woman. Every time I want a piddle, the sink's full of dirty dishes . . .

JACKIE: Hey, hold your tongue, Geordie, you'll get us chucked out . . .

MARY: Why, speak of the devil . . .

(As THOMAS enters, all spick and span.)

Where've you been all this time?

THOMAS: Been getting washed, woman, what do you think?

MARY: I think you've been playing pitch and toss with Will Jobling.

THOMAS: Would I do a thing like that, did you ever?

(He crosses to JACKIE and GEORDIE, taking out his coins as he does so. A crowd of miners gathers round.)

Wotcheor lads, are you ready?

(As they start the game, the VICAR talks to MARY.)

VICAR: Don't worry, Mrs Milburn, it's been going on for generations.

MARY: Costs a lot of money an' all.

VICAR: There was a Methodist preacher gave a famous sermon about pitch and toss . . .

MARY: Getaway.

VICAR: Over a hundred years ago.

MARY: Nothing changes.

(Rapid lighting change so that the VICAR is in a dramatic solo spot and the group of men playing pitch and toss are in semi-silhouette. Quiet chords on a church organ and the men acting out the sermon as it unfolds.)

SLIDE: 1860

VICAR (old-style Methodist): And as I walked in the street I beheld only stillness, and heard naught but the singing of birds. So I lifted mine eyes unto the hills and there I beheld a multitude. I came closer unto the multitude and may I now bear witness to what I saw upon the hillside. I beheld men of faith. In the beginning, they raised their heads and looked upwards toward Heaven with cries of 'Oh God!' . . . and then they cast their eyes downward in deep humility with cries of 'Oh Christ!' . . . Among some, there was great rejoicing, while others fell silent . . . and then let forth great shouts, invoking the name of the Lord.

(The lights revert to normal. The MEN, who have been silent throughout the sequence, let rip with their reactions to the game, carrying us into the action of the present.)

GEORDIE: You lucky devil, Tommy . . .

THOMAS: Never mind that, let's see your money . . .

JACKIE: Hey, where's your John, he likes a game?

THOMAS: He's been in bed.

MARY: Working nights, he'll be down soon.

GEORDIE: What about young Frank?

(A slight pause, a hint of tension.)

THOMAS: We'll not see him.

VICAR: Frank's your other grandson, isn't he?

MARY: Yes . . . and he'll be here, he wrote and said he would.

THOMAS: He's wrote letters before . . .

MARY: He's a busy lad.

THOMAS: Aye, and I'm a busy lad an' all . . . 'course it's a long way, all the way from Newcastle . . .

MARY: Oh, hold your tongue, man . . .

VICAR: Perhaps I shouldn't have asked.

THOMAS: She thinks the sun shines out of your Frank's . . .

VICAR: Amen.

MARY: That'll do. He was clever enough to stay out of the pit . . . and you'll not forgive anybody that . . . .

JACKIE: Howay, Tommy, don't let's be fighting . . .

GEORDIE: Why, what's a happy family without a bit of fighting?

VICAR: There's probably something in that.

GEORDIE: I mean, take my mother-in-law . . . please . . .

JACKIE: Go on . . .

GEORDIE (to audience): She's a terrible woman, my mother-in-law, a terrible woman. Been with us fourteen year, she has, fourteen terrible years . . . mind you, it's her house.

MARY: Frank'll turn up, you'll see.

THOMAS: I'll give you five to one against . . . and look you, there's no takers . . .

MARY: I remember a feller giving five to one against the King marrying Mrs Simpson . . .

THOMAS: Anyhow, shuttup about Frank, I want to enjoy myself.

(As JOHN enters.)

JOHN: Talking about Frank, are we?

THOMAS: No, we're not.

JOHN: Good.

MARY: That'll do. He is your brother.

JOHN: Aye, some say . . .

JACKIE: Working tonight, are you, John lad?

JOHN: Later on . . . like a treat to look forward to.

THOMAS: Why, he doesn't know he's bloody born.

JACKIE: Aye, that's true.

JOHN: I'll swop you your job any day, Mr Union man.

THOMAS: Gans off to work in his motor car . . .

GEORDIE: Like a merchant banker . . .

JOHN: Tell us a merchant banker goes off to work in the middle of the night.

JACKIE: You're getting well paid, lad.

JOHN: I know that . . . 'Cause I'm worth it . . .

THOMAS: Listen to the lad.

JACKIE: I wonder what Tommy Hepburn would say, hearing him talk like that.

JOHN: Who's Tommy Hepburn?

GEORDIE: Who's Tommy Hepburn, did you ever!

JOHN: Is it the cocky feller plays left-half for Sunderland?

THOMAS: He knows bonny well who he is.

JACKIE: Your first Trade Union leader, that's who he is.

MARY: Now they're off.

(MARY gets on with housewifely duties, leaving the men to get on with their reminiscences.)

JACKIE: It was Tommy Hepburn formed the first union that covered the two counties.

(A lighting change.)

JOHN: And what did he do when he'd formed it?

JACKIE: Why, man, what do you think he did? He called a bloody strike, what else?

SLIDE: 1831

March 21st, 1831, and twenty thousand miners assembled on the Town Moor to hear Thomas Hepburn speak.

SLIDE: PORTRAIT OF HEPBURN

(In the following sequence the part of HEPBURN is played by Jackie, and the three PITMEN by THOMAS, GEORDIE and JOHN respectively. The scene is punctuated by shouts and drumbeats. We see slides or film of the faces of the men to establish the sheer size of the gathering.)

HEPBURN: I am not here to make a speech. I want you lads to tell the meeting in your own words what your grievances are. Mr Charlton . . .

(As FIRST PITMAN steps forward.)

FIRST PITMAN: I just want pay for the work I do. Instead of giving it all back to the owners.

HEPBURN: How do you give it back to the owners, Mr Charlton?

FIRST PITMAN: I fill my corve . . . that's like a basket . . . with coal. There's supposed to be 7½ hundredweight of coal in it . . . if it's two pounds underweight, I don't get paid . . . if there's four pounds of stones in it . . . I . . .

HEPBURN: Four pounds out of 7½ hundredweight.

FIRST PITMAN: That's right. I filled eight baskets yesterday. I got paid for one . . . but then I got fined for not working hard enough so I ended up paying the owners.

HEPBURN: What light do you have to work by in the mine, Mr Charlton?

FIRST PITMAN: One candle.

HEPBURN: Mr Robson . . .

(SECOND PITMAN steps forward.)

SECOND PITMAN: My grievance is that I want to be paid in money . . .

HEPBURN: In money?

SECOND PITMAN: Every penny I get has to be spent at the Tommy shop . . .

HEPBURN: That's the shop that belongs to the mine owners?

SECOND PITMAN: That's right. And if there's any money owing to the shop, they deduct it from my pay . . . and now they've started paying us with tokens that have to be spent at the shop . . .

HEPBURN: And what happens if you complain about this?

SECOND PITMAN: They'll throw you out of your house . . . because your house belongs to the owners as well . . .

HEPBURN: Mr Mather.

(THIRD PITMAN steps forward.)

THIRD PITMAN: I want to know why my son should work eighteen hours a day down the pit. He gans down when it's dark, he comes up when it's dark . . . seven days a week . . . when's he going to see the sunshine?

HEPBURN: When does he go to school Mr Mather?

THIRD PITMAN: What school?

HEPBURN: How old is your son Mr Mather?

THIRD PITMAN: He's six years old, Mr Hepburn.

(HEPBURN addresses the meeting.)

HEPBURN: Lads, you know the reason for all this. We are all vicitims of the Bond . . . that piece of paper we sign once a year, agreeing to work for the owners on their terms. And you've heard what their terms mean.

(Crowd reaction.)

Lads, you will be asked to sign your next annual bond on April 5th. We will refuse, each and every one of us, until the owners meet our demands.

(Reactions.)

We are demanding a twelve-hour working day for boys. We are demanding that our wages be paid in money, and that we be free to spend that money wherever we please.

(Reactions.)

The men of each colliery will meet twice a week, each colliery to send a delegate to a central committee. Each of us will subscribe sixpence so we can send petitioners to Parliament, to plead our case. All in favour of these resolutions?

(A massive shout of approval.)

Lads . . . to know how to wait is the secret of success. The time will come when the golden chain that binds the tyrants together will be snapped; when men will be properly organised; when coal owners will be like ordinary men and will have to sigh for the days gone by.

(A cheer dying down as the lights revert to normal.)

JOHN: And what happened? (Sceptical.)

THOMAS: There was a great strike in 1831, another one in 1832.

JOHN: Aye, but what happened?

THOMAS: Oh, the coal owners called in the military, there was a lot of fighting, couple of murders . . .

GEORDIE: Just a big party, that's all.

JOHN: What did you achieve?

JACKIE: The owners agreed a twelve-hour day for boys of six years old.

GEORDIE: And the conscience of the nation was stirred, never forget that.

JOHN: All agreed on paper?

JACKIE: Don't be daft, man, they never agreed anything on paper . . . the Union wasn't recognised.

THOMAS: We had to take the word of the coal owners . . .

JACKIE: As aristocrats and gentlemen.

(Pause.)

THOMAS: Aye.

GEORDIE: Aye.

JACKIE: Aye.

THOMAS: That really was a Union. It's all different now.

JACKIE: That's true enough.

(And Jackie sings his song.)

When that I was and a little tiny boy,
Me daddy said to me,
'The time has come, me bonny bonny bairn
To learn your ABC.'
Now Daddy was a Lodge Chairman
In the coalfields of the Tyne
And that ABC was different
From the Enid Blyton kind.

He sang:

A is for Alienation that made me the man that I am
and B's for the Boss who's a bastard, a bourgeois who don't give a damn.
C is for Capitalism, the boss's reactionary creed
and D's for Dictatorship, laddie, but the best proletarian breed.
E is for Exploitation that the workers have suffered so long
and F is for Old Ludwig Feuerbach, the first one to see it was wrong.
G is for all Gerrymanderers like Lord Muck and Sir Whatsisname
and H is the Hell that they'll go to, when the workers have kindled the flame.
I is for Imperialism and America's kind is the worst
and J is for sweet Jingoism that the Tories all think of first.

K is for good old Keir Hardie who fought out the working class fight
and L is for Vladimir Lenin who showed him the Left was all right.
M is of course for Karl Marx the daddy and mammy of them all
and N is for Nationalisation, without it we'd crumble and fall.
O is for Over-production that capitalist economy brings
and P is for all private property – the greatest of all of the sins.
Q is for Quid pro quo that we'll deal out so well and so soon
when R for Revolution is shouted and the Red Flag becomes the top
tune.
S is for sad Stalinism that gave us all such a bad name
and T is for Trotsky the hero who had to take all of the blame.
U's for the Union of workers, the Union will stand to the end.
and V is for Vodka, yes, Vodka, the one drink that don't bring the bends.
W is for all Willing workers and that's where the memory fades
for X Y and Z, me dear daddy said, will be written on the street barricades.

But now that I'm not a little tiny boy
Me daddy says to me,
'Please try to forget the things I said,
Especially the ABC.'
For Daddy's no longer a Union man
And he's had to change his plea.
His alphabet is different now
Since they made him a Labour MP.

(FRANK and RUTH enter towards the end of the song. They join the
on-stage applause and then the others realise they have arrived.)

MARY: Frank, pet . . .

(MARY and FRANK embrace.)

FRANK: Hello, Grandma . . .

THOMAS: Condescended to come, then . . .

FRANK: Did you think I wouldn't?

JOHN: You wouldn't dare stay away.

FRANK: There you are, Granda . . . Johnny Walker's golden best.

(He gives THOMAS a bottle of whisky.)

THOMAS: Ta. (Almost grateful.)

FRANK: You're looking fit, John.

JOHN: It's all the sunshine and fresh air. You're looking very pale yourself.

FRANK: Late nights and drinking out of wet glasses.

(He introduces RUTH, who looks a slightly alien element in this context.)

This is Ruth . . . my grandmother . . .

MARY: Hello, pet.

FRANK: My big brother, John.

RUTH: Hello, John.

JOHN: Hello, Ruth.

FRANK: My grandfather . . .

THOMAS: Grandfather? Did you ever . . . hello, pet.

RUTH: Nice to meet you, I've heard a lot about you.

MARY: It's all true.

THOMAS: You're courting, are you, you two?

FRANK: You might say.

RUTH: Sort of.

THOMAS: Sort of! I always knew if I was bloody well courting.

GEORDIE: My father used to say to me, 'Never start courting, lad, and bring your children up the same way.'

JACKIE: That's immoral.

VICAR: But you can't help laughing . . .

JACKIE: You are at the college as well, are you, pet?

RUTH: Post-graduate research, the same as Frank.

JACKIE: I'll believe you, even if I don't know what it means.

GEORDIE: Sounds dirty to me.

MARY: Everything sounds dirty to you.

GEORDIE: Never you mind, I've heard a few things about Newcastle . . . Jesmond Road especially, all mink coats and no knickers . . .

MARY: Pay no attention to him, I'm glad you both came . . .

FRANK: I bet they've all been having a good crack.

MARY: They never stop.

FRANK: Tommy Hepburn?

JOHN: What do you know about Tommy Hepburn?

FRANK: Well, him and them other Union leaders, they fought for education for the miners . . . he gave me my chance in a way, didn't he?

JOHN: He missed me, didn't he?

THOMAS: You're getting educated at the coal face, that's the best education of all.

JOHN: Anyways, who wants to talk about ancient history, what's the matter with football and dogs . . ?

GEORDIE: Did I tell you Joe Pattinson's got hisself a new dog?

JACKIE: Oh, aye, what sort?

GEORDIE: He says it's an African whippet . . .

JACKIE: An African whippet?

GEORDIE: I says to him, it looks a bit fierce, Joe . . . yes, he says, it's been like that since we cut his mane off.

JOHN (to THOMAS): What about your fight?

MARY: Which one? Fighting all the time . . .

JOHN: The big one . . .

MARY: Nobody wants to hear about it.

THOMAS: Me and Will Jobling?

FRANK: Your mate?

THOMAS: Him that's down there now, looking after the pumps.

MARY (to audience): I'm married to it. Wake us up when he finishes.

(A single spot on THOMAS.)

THOMAS: Getting on for fifty years ago, and me and Will was working in the thin seam . . . maybe two foot high, six foot across . . . thin and wet . . .

(A soft light on JOHN and FRANK re-creating the situation. The tiredness, the tension and the claustrophobia.)

And hot . . . getting towards the end of the shift and it's like a furnace . . . so I reach out for a drink of water . . . and there's none there . . .

(A long silent pause between the two men.)

Will had drunk my water. Must have been an accident because he'd never do a thing like that . . . except that this time he did it . . . and that meant he'd have to pay. So comes the end of the day, we find worselves a referee and it's back of the tip we go . . .

(JOHN and FRANK prepare for the fight, JOHN as THOMAS, FRANK as JOBLING. JACKIE is the referee, GEORDIE the bookie. The others gather round. The fight is dramatic and stylised, reflecting THOMAS's account throughout.)

'Course I was bigger than him, but he was light and fit and fast on his feet . . . and he had good lungs in them days . . .

GEORDIE: Six to four on Milburn, evens Jobling . . .

THOMAS: And at the first, he had the best of it . . .

GEORDIE: Six to four on Jobling, evens Milburn . . .

THOMAS: In fact, you'll never believe it but he knocked us down once . . .

(MILBURN down.)

GEORDIE: Five to one Milburn, I'm not laying Jobling . . .

THOMAS: But as I say, I was stronger than him . . .

(MILBURN gets up and starts to take the fight to JOBLING.)

And he had drunk my water. I think that's what made the difference, really . . . having right on my side.

VICAR: It does help.

(MILBURN drives JOBLING round the ring.)

GEORDIE: Threes Jobling, two to one on Milburn.

THOMAS: But he wouldn't stay down.

(JOBLING down and up.)

So what could I do? I just had to keep hitting him.

GEORDIE: Sixes Jobling, anybody wants sixes Jobling? . . I divven blame you . . .

THOMAS: And then in the end . . .

GEORDIE: No more bets.

THOMAS: He stayed down.

(JOBLING stays down.)

By God, he was a mess. And not a mark on me.

MARY: So he told me . . . walked into a wall, he said . . .

THOMAS: You're wrong, woman.

MARY: Or got a black eye shaving, I forget which.

(JOBLING gets up, helped by MILBURN. The crowd breaks up and the two of them walk off together.)

THOMAS: If you're a man, you've got to fight.

MARY: Whatever for?

THOMAS: That's how you find out who your friends are.

(The party is resumed.)

GEORDIE (to the audience): I lost a packet on that . . . it's real money we're using, you know . . . they'll cash it at the Co-op . . .

VICAR: Of course, there isn't so much fighting now, is there?

JOHN: You don't see it so much . . .

THOMAS: But it still goes on . . . right, John?

JOHN: Oh, aye, it still goes on.

(JOHN and THOMAS exchange a look of mutual knowledge and understanding.)

JACKIE: There was more important fights than that one, though.

JOHN: Getaway.

JACKIE: Like in 1844.

THOMAS: The Great Strike.

JOHN: Not another bloody strike.

FRANK: Another bloody strike, yes . . .

JOHN: What the hell d'you know about it? . . .

(And a moment of tension between the brothers.)

RUTH: Oh, stoppit, the two of you!

MARY: Good lass.

JOHN (to RUTH): Your business, is it?

RUTH: Only me knows that.

JOHN: I think I'll open that bottle of whisky you brought, young Frank.

(A roll of drums and a lighting change.)

SLIDE: 1844.

(In the strike sequence, all the parts are played by those on-stage, with simple costume changes – a hat, a coat, a cloak, shawls and scarves for the women.)

JACKIE: Strike meeting, Shadon's Hill, 1844, forty thousand men present. Their leader, Mr Martin Jude.

(THOMAS as MARTIN JUDE.)

JUDE: If we have come to the field of battle, let us fight nobly and the day will be ours.

(A persistent drumbeat under JUDE's speech, leading into the song to come.)

All the employers think about is getting as much work done for as little pay as possible and when they are not able to go any further, they turn us out of doors. Brothers, the employers want to reduce our wages. Do we agree to this?

(A shout of 'No'.)

They think we are ignorant. Well, if we are ignorant, what is the cause? Have those who profit from our labours done anything towards our education? What school accommodation was ever provided for workers' children? The owners sink a shaft and build hovels for workmen to live in. Those who have children are housed on the same principle as those who have none. I know of families with seven and eight children grown up to men and women in one small space . . . four yards by five yards . . . the miner's castle . . .

(The song starts, in chorus.)

ALL:
Time for to make a stand, me lads,
Time for to take a hand, me lads,
Time for us to unite, me lads,
Time for to start a fight, me lads.

Time, Time, Time,
Time for to get the pitman some justice and peace.

JUDE (speaks over music link, instrumental only): Brothers, it's time to say to the Lords and Masters, we want paying for the work we do, a fair rate, not a penny less, and no more cheating by the managers.

ALL:
Time for to make a stand, me lads,
Time for to take a hand, me lads,
Time for us to unite, me lads,
Time for to start a fight, me lads.
Time, Time, Time,
Time for to get the pitman some justice and peace.

JUDE: Brothers, it's time to end the killing and the maiming, it's time for proper safety precautions, it's time to end legalised murder in the name of profit.

ALL:
Time for to make a stand, me lads,
Time for to take a hand, me lads,
Time for us to unite, me lads,
Time for to start a fight, me lads,
Time, Time, Time,
Time for to get the pitman some justice and peace.

JUDE: Brothers, it is time to say this is the end of our slavery, this is the end of our bondage.

ALL:
Time for to make a stand, me lads,
Time for to take a hand, me lads,
Time for us to unite, me lads,
Time for to start a fight, me lads,
Time, Time, Time,
Time for to get the pitman some justice and peace.

JUDE: Brothers, I ask you not to break the peace. I ask you to stand faithfully by your Union. I ask you to separate from this meeting in a peacable manner. I beg you, at all times keep the peace or you will smash the Union.

(A quiet dispersal. The EXPERT comes in, as LORD LONDONDERRY.)

LONDONDERRY: Of course, this is all very moving but you must realise there are two sides to this question.

JACKIE: Lord Londonderry, coal owner and gentleman . . .

LONDONDERRY: The most deluded and obstinate victim of designing men must now perceive that they cannot become masters and dictate terms to the coal owners. Already 3639 are employed, principally strangers to the district, in hewing coals. And sensible men have left the Union and returned to work. Pitmen, I enjoin! I conjure you! to look upon the ruin you are bringing on your wives, your children, your county and your country. I gave you two weeks to consider whether you would return to work before I proceeded to eject you from your houses. I found you dogged, obstinate and determined . . . indifferent to my really paternal advice and kind feelings.

VICAR: The Epistle of St James, Chapter Five. Go to now, ye rich men, weep and howl for the miseries that shall come upon you.

LONDONDERRY: I was bound to act up to my word, bound by duty to my property, my family and my station.

VICAR: Your silver and gold is cankered, and the rush of them shall be a witness against you and shall consume your flesh as it were fire.

LONDONDERRY: I have now brought forty Irishmen to the pits, and if, by the thirteenth of the month, a large body of pitmen do not return to their labour, I will obtain one hundred more, and proceed to eject that number, who are now illegally and unjustly in the possession of my houses, and in the following week a further one hundred shall follow.

(Fade out light on LONDONDERRY so that the stage is in darkness. There is a loud hammering. Fade up lights on the house which is now a pitman's house of the period. In it a PITMAN and his WIFE are sleeping, and an OLD LADY, and a BABY in a cot. The adult parts are played by FRANK, RUTH and MARY. The hammering is repeated and the lights go up to reveal a POLICEMAN, accompanied by a couple of villainous looking BAILIFFS and a SOLDIER. The PITMAN gets up and opens the door. The POLICEMAN comes in, the others following. A group of PITMEN and WIVES gathers outside.)

POLICEMAN: Will you gan to work?

(The PITMAN looks round the room.)

Will you gan to work?

(He looks at his WIFE, who looks away.)

For the third time. Will you gan to work?

(Pause.)

JUDE (in separate spot): I beg you, at all times, keep the peace or you will smash the Union.

PITMAN: No.

(The eviction proceeds. All the furniture — what there is — is carried outside, where it is deposited roughly. The WIFE takes the baby carefully. Outside, the watchers help to arrange the furniture in a rough square, then throw a canvas sheet over the top to keep out the rain. The evicted family huddle beneath it. As the eviction nears completion they all turn to watch the owners' men, and start a slow handclapping, augmented by pots and pans, which reaches a rapid, deafening climax. Then stops with a sudden bang silence.)

VICAR: Ye have lived in pleasure on the earth and been wanton; ye have nourished your hearts as in the day of slaughter; ye have condemned and killed the just; and he doth not resist you.

LONDONDERRY: Believe me, I am your sincere friend, Lord Londonderry.

JUDE (off): 35,000 men, women and children were evicted in Northumberland and Durham during the 1844 strike.

LONDONDERRY: Your sincere friend.

VICAR: Be patient therefore, brethren, unto the coming of the Lord.

JACKIE: After twenty weeks on strike the following resolution was carried at meetings throughout the two counties.

JUDE: Seeing the present state of things, and being compelled to retreat from the field through the overbearing cruelty of our employers, the suffering of our families, and the treachery of those who have been at work during the strike, we at the present time deem it necessary to make the best terms with the employers we can. Agreed?

(Slowly the hands go up.)

It is resolved that no single individual shall go to the colliery office for work, but that all shall go in a body and meet the resident viewer. Agreed?

(Again the hands go up. A group of miners cross the stage and meet LONDONDERRY and his MANAGER.)

MANAGER: Now, lads, I suppose you request an interview with me?

(They nod, almost imperceptibly.)

I know what conclusion you have come to. You mean to commence on the employers' terms. Well . . . things will be just the same as they were before you left work . . . just the same . . .

(The men look up and there is a spark of rebellion, but silent.)

JUDE (off): I beg you at all times, keep the peace, or you will smash the Union.

MANAGER: Just the same.

(A pause, then the MANAGER turns and goes off, the men following. LONDONDERRY watches, smiling, then follows them. One of the WIVES moves forward and sings. Behind her, the young PITMAN, his WIFE and the OLD WOMAN move back into the house. They have no furniture left to speak of, and no baby. During the WIFE's song, the song the men sung at the strike meeting is heard as a counter-melody, quietly, but persistent.)

WIFE (sings):
    Twenty long weeks, twenty long weeks,
    bonny black bird, twenty long weeks,
    Singin' that song, like nothin' was wrong,
    haven't you heard? Twenty long weeks.

    Twenty long weeks, twenty long weeks,
    canny black bird, twenty long weeks,
    Yon soft feathered breast, may warm the bairns' nest
    But my bairn lies dead; twenty long weeks.

    Twenty long weeks, twenty long weeks,
    fly away high, twenty long weeks,
    and birdie take care, there's hawks in the air,
    and not only there; twenty long weeks.

    (By the end of the song, the stage is in darkness except for a light on the
    WIFE. This fades out as the lights fade up on the party scene, still bright
    but thoughtful now.)

JACKIE: No, lad, there's never been a strike like that one.

MARY: You sound sorry about it . . .

JACKIE: No, I'm not sorry. There was over much suffering . . .

GEORDIE: There was some that died.

THOMAS: Plenty.

MARY: My granda was in it . . .

JACKIE: What happened to him?

MARY: He was a Union man . . . he didn't get his job back.

FRANK: I thought there was no victimisation.

JACKIE: They always *say* that.

MARY: He went on the parish.

GEORDIE: So this woman come knocking at me door, says we're taking
    a collection for the workhouse, hev you got owt for us? Why, aye, I
    says, wait there, I'll gan and fetch wor lass . . .

FRANK: They brought in a lot of Welsh and Irish didn't they? In the strike?

THOMAS: Hundreds.

FRANK: What happened to them?

THOMAS: Most of them went home again . . . like gentle reason prevailed . . .

JACKIE: They were shown the error of their ways . . .

RUTH: No victimisation?

THOMAS: Persuasion, that's all, hinny . . . persuasion . . .

RUTH (to MARY): Are they always like this?

MARY: Like what, pet?

RUTH: Living in the past?

THOMAS: What's the matter with the lass?

MARY: She wants to know if you always live in the past. I told her yes.

VICAR: That's brave talk.

THOMAS: Well, we've had a bigger ration of past here than most places . . .

JACKIE: And there's great traditions.

RUTH: You could make new traditions . . .

JACKIE: If you're talking about building for the future, I agree with you, but you've got to study the past first . . . like pick the teams . . . see who's on your side . . . and who isn't.

RUTH: But things have changed . . . I mean people care . . .

JACKIE: Which people?

RUTH: Well . . . the top people . . .

JACKIE: Read the top people's newspaper . . . Colour supplement, business supplement, art supplement . . .

GEORDIE: By God, I didn't think they had a supplement for *that*!

JACKIE: It's to prove they care, Geordie . . .

CHORUS (JACKIE and GEORDIE — both armed with a colour supplement):
Somebody cares, somebody cares
So nice to know, lads
That Somebody cares.

JACKIE:
Just pick up your supplement.

GEORDIE:
See how they care.

JACKIE:
The good things of life, lads

GEORDIE:
They want you to share.

JACKIE:
Brand new Cortinas

GEORDIE:
And Washin' Machines

JACKIE:
Wall to Wall Carpets

GEORDIE:
And tins o' Bile Beans

CHORUS (JACKIE and GEORDIE):
Somebody cares, somebody cares

So nice to know, lads
That Somebody cares.

JACKIE:
Fly to Majorca

GEORDIE:
In a swish V.C.10

JACKIE:
Oil Central Heating

GEORDIE:
When you come home again.

JACKIE:
Smoke Rothman King Size

GEORDIE:
With Labour let's go

JACKIE:
Your best friend will tell you

GEORDIE (sniff, sniff, sniff):
B.O.

CHORUS (JACKIE and GEORDIE):
Somebody cares, somebody cares.
So nice to know, lads
That Somebody cares

GEORDIE:
Look at the headlines

JACKIE:
Stock markets boom

GEORDIE:
Dividends doubled

JACKIE:
North-East in gloom

GEORDIE:
Labour queues lengthen

JACKIE (excited):
But Geordie, see this,
Power Station for Teesside —

GEORDIE (speaks): Had on a bit. Jackie — yon's a Nuclear Power Station.
Doesn't need no coal.

JACKIE (speaks): That's what I'm tellin' ye, Geordie . . .

CHORUS (JACKIE and GEORDIE):
Somebody cares, somebody cares
So nice to know, lads

That Somebody cares.

JACKIE:
  So if you want us to think about tomorrow . . . have a look at today first.

FRANK: You're still fighting Lord Londonderry?

JACKIE: Aye, he keeps changing his name but . . .

THOMAS: Anyways, don't go asking a pitman to think about tomorrow . . .

RUTH: Why not?

THOMAS: Because, pet, . . . it doesn't always arrive.

JOHN: She's dead right.

FRANK: Is she really?

JOHN: Yes, she is really.

RUTH: Thank you.

VICAR: You're going to start a fight, John.

JOHN: I should worry. I can beat anybody here.

FRANK: In what way is Ruth right?

JOHN: What I mean is, I'm sick of all the stories about the pitmen getting a good hiding . . . Tell us a story where the pitmen won, for God's sake . . .

JACKIE: They won in 1872.

THOMAS: That's right.

  (A light change.)

JACKIE: On August 10th, 1872 the Coal Mines Regulation Bill became law.

  (As the men speak, we hear quiet drumbeats building up to the single chorus at the end of the sequence.)

FIRST PITMAN: No boy under the age of ten, and no girl or woman of any age shall be employed in any coalmine.

ALL: Time for to make a stand, me lads.

SECOND PITMAN: Boys of the age of ten shall not be employed in any mine unless such labour be necessary by reason of the thinness of the seam.

ALL: Time for to take a hand, me lads.

FIRST PITMAN: The boy shall not work more than six hours in the day, and not more than six days in any one week . . . if he works less than six days in the week, he may work up to ten hours in any one day . . .

ALL: Time for us to unite, me lads.

SECOND PITMAN: Boys aged between twelve and sixteen shall work below ground not more than fifty-four hours in a week and not more than ten hours in any one day.

ALL: Time for to start a fight, lads.

FIRST PITMAN: Every boy aged twelve to thirteen shall attend school at least twenty hours in a fortnight, Sundays not being included.

ALL: Time . . .

SECOND PITMAN: The system of working mines with single shafts is abolished.

ALL: Time . . .

FIRST PITMAN: All coal shall be paid for by weight instead of by measure.

ALL: Time . . .

SECOND PITMAN: The owners shall make returns of all coal raised yearly out of their mines, and also a return of all lives lost, and all personal injury sustained by explosions, inundations or accidents of whatever nature.

ALL: Time for to get the pitman some justice and peace.

(Pause.)

FIRST PITMAN: In this way Parliament recognised all the main grievances of the Miners' Unions.

THOMAS: Like Tommy Hepburn said . . . forty years previous . . . to know how to wait is the secret of success.

(And a lighting link back into the present but less abrupt than previous links — the two are more or less as one till the end of the act.)

VICAR: It was a long time to wait, forty years . . .

FRANK: And then for what?

JACKIE: A thirty-six-hour week for lads of ten . . . a fifty-four-hour week for lads of twelve . . .

FRANK: You see what I mean?

JACKIE: We'd got something down on paper, Frank lad, and that had never happened before . . .

THOMAS: And the rulers of the land had listened to the working man, and that had never happened before . . .

GEORDIE: And we'd stirred the conscience of the Nation, and that had never happened before . . . well, not much . . .

FRANK: What about Lord Londonderry?

JACKIE: Still there.

GEORDIE: I mean, the way I look at it is, like it wasn't the end, or even the beginning of the middle of the end, or even the start of the beginning of the middle of the end . . . but . . .

JACKIE: Gan on . . .

GEORDIE: More like the start of the middle of the beginning.

JACKIE: Only not in so many words.

THOMAS: And Tommy Hepburn, the lad that started it, he died the year after the Mines Bill was passed . . . died a poor man . . .

JACKIE: But he'd seen what he was fighting for come to pass.

VICAR: After forty years.

JACKIE: It was a long forty years for Tommy.

THOMAS: It was forty long years for everybody.

GEORDIE: Howay, this is supposed to be a fifty-year celebration not a forty-year wake!

THOMAS: Aye, but it's a grand old story. What d'you think of that, wor John?

JOHN: Well, to tell you the truth I didn't hear a bloody word.

GEORDIE: C'mon, Vic, get those bottles out . . . Don't worry, you can go for one yourselves in a minute . . .

SONG:
  Let's drink to the Union, the Union, the Union,
  The Union that's strong as a good pint of beer.

GEORDIE:
  Downstairs in the bar they've got pints lined up waiting
  As soon as you supped them we'll see you back here.

ALL:
  So drink to the Union, the Union, the Union.
  As soon as you've supped them, we'll see you back here.

ACT TWO

The stage is in total darkness.

THOMAS: The thin seam. You take a lamp, into the most terrifying darkness, and you are not afraid.

(And slowly a soft light fades up on THOMAS and the highlights of one or two people gathered round him to listen — FRANK included. As he continues his story, four miners crawl on from the opposite side of the stage, out of and into the darkness, enacting the story. All we see is their lamps.)

You meet a darkness like a velvet pad pressed against your open eye. At two hundred fathoms the sun takes no levy nor gives of his majesty. Only a memory of him and the urge to return quickly.

FRANK: What happened?

THOMAS: First comes the noise.

(A dull roar building up.)

The noise but no understanding — only the need to escape from the noise, the urge to run but there's no running in the thin seam.

(The men trying to get away, speed and urgency without movement, as in a nightmare.)

Only the crawling and the tearing and the noise, all of us, me and Will, Jimmy and Art, and the noise . . .

(The noise reaches a climax. One of the lamps is extinguished. A loud cry diminishing to silence.)

It is finished.

FRANK: Then what?

THOMAS: Then you count heads . . . one, two, three . . . no fourth. No Jimmy.

FRANK: Dead?

THOMAS: Caught by the noise.

FRANK: Can you be sure in the dark?

THOMAS: You can be sure.

FRANK: In the dark? In the thin seam?

THOMAS: There, in the thin seam, where the roof and the floor meet like the jaws of a vice, there were two hands, the fingers arched so that the nails dug into the dust. You can be sure.

(A pause. Then a cross-fade to JOHN and RUTH standing outside the house. Very casual — deliberate contrast to previous sequence — maybe they are lighting cigarettes.)

RUTH: Why come out here?

JOHN: The stories.

RUTH: Your grandfather's stories?

JOHN: I've heard them all before.

RUTH: They're marvellous stories.

JOHN: Oh, aye.

RUTH: To somebody like me.

JOHN: That's right. Somebody like you.

(Pause.)

RUTH: What's the matter with me?

JOHN: You're a bonny lass, nowt the matter with that.

RUTH: You should be proud of the stories.

JOHN: Stuff them.

RUTH: Why?

JOHN: Because, me bonny lass, in the middle of the night when other folks is in bed, I'm off into the pit to earn my bread and butter. I don't need no bloody stories to remind us what it's all about.

(Cross-fade to the scene as before. THOMAS telling the story, and the miners crouching in the darkness.)

THOMAS: The bare rock is not tender and returns blow for blow with sudden sharpness. The Lord broods over the depths and men disturb his brooding, to pay in passion and the sweat and blood of their bodies.

FRANK: In the thin seam.

THOMAS: The thin seam, yes. Men do this. My people, your people. They pierce the fabric of his temple; make an incision into the heart of his mystery. At the same time, unthinkingly, they tend the hem of his robe and make most glorious the thin seam of his garment.

(Pause.)

MARY: Get on with the story, man, I want to make a cup of tea.

THOMAS: We kept on crawling for about three days and three nights, till we came out at the colliery at Jawblades . . . walked all the way back here to Brockenback, just in time for the funeral procession for the lads that didn't get out, like . . .

FRANK: What did you do?

THOMAS: Why man, we tagged on behind, all in wor dirt, then afterwards we all had a good swill down, then we went out and got blind drunk.

(Raucous reaction from the guests. The miners enacting the story get up, relax, smile and stroll off the stage. Lights up brighter on the party.)

MARY: By, you tell a canny tale, Thomas Milburn.

THOMAS: True, every last word, you ask Will Jobling . . .

JACKIE: It's all recorded history.

GEORDIE: I believe you, sure as I'm riding this chariot.

FRANK: It's a great story.

THOMAS: If you really think that, fill us up, lad . . .

FRANK: I really think that.

(Cross-fade to JOHN and RUTH.)

JOHN: You look all wrong, don't you?

RUTH: Thank you very much.

JOHN: Standing there, wearing that dress, and the slagheap behind . . . they divven match up.

RUTH: Whose fault's that?

JOHN: Always asking questions . . .

RUTH: Only because I want to know the answers.

JOHN: Ask the right questions. Ask me where's my mam and dad.

RUTH: Where are they?

JOHN: My dad got killed in the pit when I was five . . . just him on his own, it wasn't what they call a disaster, no headlines, no appeal funds . . . just him . . . my mam died of TB couple of years after . . . one of the great things about pit villages . . .

RUTH: What?

JOHN: Better chance of dying of rotten lungs than anywhere else in England.

(Pause.)

RUTH: Actually, I knew about your parents.

JOHN: Did you . . . actually?

RUTH: Frank told me.

JOHN: Oh, him.

RUTH: What do you mean . . . oh, him?

JOHN: Well he cleared off, didn't he?

(Cross-fade to the party.)

FRANK: I think it's time we had some toasts.

GEORDIE: Never mind the toasts, let's get on with the boozin' . . .

VICAR: Let us now praise famous men . . .

GEORDIE: My old mother, she's ninety-six and never used glasses in her life . . . straight out the bottle . . .

MARY: They're away now, their feet'll not touch the floor till the morning . . .

JACKIE: There's only one toast . . . the Union of workers . . .

ALL: The Union of workers . . .

(They drink the toast .As they do so, one of the WIVES steps forward to sing.)

WIFE (sings):
My old man's a Union man
As happy as happy can be
He spends his life on a piece-work plan
But it brings no peace to me.
When he comes home at the break of dawn
He gives to me this greetin':
Mary dear, ye've nowt to fear – I've been to a Union meetin'.

My old man's a Union man
As jolly as jolly can be.
He's working now on an overtime ban
But he finds no time for me.
When he comes home tight on a Friday night
He says he's not been cheating
An' he's not been drinkin', oh dear no,
He's been to a Union meeting.

My old man's a Union man
As bonny as bonny can be
But once in a while he's a family man
And he stays at home wi' me.
And he takes his turns and he minds the bairns
And then he starts repeatin':
'Tonight's the night, turn out the light'
(spoken: 'Ooh, hinnies'.)
That's a lovely Union meeting.

(Song ends. Reactions and applause out of which the VICAR's voice emerges.)

VICAR: If I might break in . . .

GEORDIE: Aye, gan on, Vic . . .

VICAR: I'd like to propose a toast . . .

GEORDIE: And then we'll take a collection for the belfry . . .

JACKIE: Shuttup, man, you're showing your ignorance . . .

GEORDIE: Well, why shouldn't I? I'm as ignorant as the next man.

VICAR: I'd like to propose a toast to the happy couple, Mr and Mrs Milburn . . .

ALL: Mr and Mrs Milburn . . .

VICAR: And that far-off day when they decided to tread the path of matrimony . . .

MARY: In 1918.

(Pause.)

THOMAS: 1918 . . .

(They drink the toast and a sudden hush.)

SLIDE: 1918.

(Then film or stills of the period. Music of the time, perhaps on a harmonica.)

Well, you see, in 1918, we'd just had this big war. And the country needed lots of coal to fight the war and it turned out the coal owners weren't clever enough to organise it properly . . . so the Government took over all the mines.

(During the following sequence, the men put on hats appropriate to the parts they are playing — cloth caps for the Union of workers, bowlers for the politicians, toppers for the coal owners.)

JACKIE: Like nationalisation?

THOMAS: Like nationalisation, aye . . . and come the end of the war and the coal owners come to Lloyd George and they say . . .

GEORDIE: Please can we hev wor coal mines back, please?

THOMAS: And Lloyd George says . . . can ye, hell . . . and then the coal owners say . . .

GEORDIE: What about wor poor bairns running barefoot in South Kensington?

THOMAS: And Lloyd George says, we'll have a Royal Commission.

(Fanfare.)

Led by the honourable Mr Sankey . . . hey, Mr Sankey!

(JACKIE as SANKEY.)

JACKIE: What is it, David lad?

THOMAS: I'd like yes to hev a Royal Commission.

JACKIE: Righto.

(to the audience): So me and twelve other wise men gans down the pub and we talk it over and then we decided . . .

(JACKIE has a brief chat with three of the men. He turns to THOMAS.)

We've decided, Mr Lloyd George.

THOMAS: What have ye decided, Mr Sankey?

JACKIE: We think you ought to nationalise the coalmines.

(Pause. LLOYD GEORGE is shaken.)

THOMAS: Now hang on a bit, lad . . . I'm not sure that's what we wanted you to think . . . who've you got on your team?

JACKIE: Well, there's three Union men . . . they want nationalisation.

THOMAS: Well, we cannot trust them . . . who else?

JACKIE: Well, there's three socialist sympathisers . . . they want nationalisation.

THOMAS: Well, we certainly cannot trust them . . . who else?

JACKIE: There's three coal owners . . . they divven want nationalisation . . .

THOMAS: Well, I divven trust them but I dorsen't say so, not out loud . . . who else?

JACKIE: Three great industrialists.

THOMAS: Oh, that's good, you can certainly trust great industrialists . . . and what did they say?

JACKIE: They divven want nationalisation.

THOMAS: Good lads.

JACKIE: So that left me with the casting vote, and I voted in favour.

THOMAS: Ye what?

JACKIE: I voted in favour.

THOMAS: Right, the Royal Commission's against nationalisation.

JACKIE: But it wasn't, it was in favour.

THOMAS: The impartial ones was against it.

JACKIE: Who says great industrialists are impartial?

THOMAS: Me, Lloyd George says it . . . and you look in the papers in the morning . . . Believe me, Mr Sankey, I speak as the man whose hand is firmly steering the helm of the ship of state through turbulent waters . . .

JACKIE: Oh, the fine eloquence of the Welsh!

THOMAS: And another thing, Mr Sankey . . .

JACKIE: What is it, David lad?

THOMAS: That's the last bloody Royal Commission you get out of me.

JACKIE: Right lads . . . off you go . . .

(The Royal Commission departs.)

GEORDIE: Please can we have our coalmines back, please?

THOMAS: Yes, you can, if you promise to be good . . .

GEORDIE: Why, aye, we'll promise to be good.

JACKIE: And that was the first mistake.

THOMAS: And what had you in mind as your first contribution to the national well-being?

GEORDIE: We thought we'd cut the wages of the miners.

THOMAS: So they cut the wages.

JACKIE: And we wouldn't accept the wage cut.

GEORDIE: So we locked them out for three months.

JACKIE: And at the end of three months . . . we went back to work.

GEORDIE: And we cut their wages.

(Fanfare.)

SLIDE: 1925

FRANK: 1925.

GEORDIE: Stanley Baldwin.

JACKIE: Oh, aye, I remember Stanley Baldwin.

GEORDIE: One of the canniest little fellers you'd never want to meet again.

(ALL as themselves now.)

THOMAS: Hey, and you knaw what happened in 1925.

(Fanfare.)

ALL: Britain gans back onto the Gold Standard.

(Pause.)

GEORDIE: Britain gans back onto the Gold Standard.

JACKIE: That's right . . .

GEORDIE: What the hell's it mean?

(EXPERT comes on, with the VICAR on his knee as a ventriloquist's dummy.)

EXPERT: Perhaps I can help you there . . .

JACKIE: Gan on . . .

EXPERT: The Government of 1925 was anxious to maintain the strength of sterling.

GEORDIE: Oh, aye, that's important, we all believe in that, right, lads?

THOMAS: Oh, aye.

JACKIE: Certainly.

EXPERT: So the then Chancellor of the Exchequer . . . Mr Churchill . . .

(Reactions.)

GEORDIE: Would that be . . . Winston Churchill?

EXPERT: Of course . . . something the matter?

(Pause.)

THOMAS: Get on with the pound sterling.

EXPERT: The Chancellor thought it right to stabilise the value of the pound . . . by revaluing it some ten per cent higher than previously.

(FRANK breaks in, as cross talk comedian.)

FRANK: I say, I say, I say. Was this to put the economy back on its feet again?

VICAR (as dummy): Exactly.

FRANK: Give the country a fresh chance in world markets?

VICAR (as dummy): Precisely.

FRANK: Re-establish our world role?

VICAR (as dummy): Absolutely.

FRANK: But I thought you did that by de-valuation . . . by reducing its value, rather than increasing it.

VICAR (as dummy): Well . . . you, can, of course, do either . . . it simply depends . . . what you believe in . . .

GEORDIE: By God, it takes a clever dummy to talk rubbish like that.

EXPERT: The situation demanded action!

(To FRANK): We could use a young chap like you on our side.

JACKIE: But hang on a minute . . . if you increase the value of the pound . . . that means the stuff we export is going to cost more . . .

EXPERT: All our exports will cost our customers ten per cent more.

THOMAS: Including coal.

EXPERT: Yes, we do export a certain amount of coal. That will cost overseas customers ten per cent more.

THOMAS: Aye.

EXPERT: Unless.

THOMAS: Unless?

EXPERT: Unless we can drastically cut production costs and thus maintain present prices.

THOMAS: And then the coal owners thought of a great way of cutting production costs.

GEORDIE (as coal owner): We'll cut the miners' wages by ten per cent!

(Fanfare.)

JACKIE (as Union man): Ye'll dae nothing of the sort . . .

VICAR (as dummy): The country does rely on the co-operation of all sections of industry in this, our great hour of need . . . saw your lips move.

THOMAS: Oh, hadaway to Hell!

(EXPERT goes off, with dummy.)

I, Stanley Baldwin, will settle this.

GEORDIE: The situation is menacing, Stanley.

THOMAS: Aye, it is, lad. But I know what to do about it. We'll hev a Royal Commission!

(Fanfare.)

JACKIE: And the world breathed again.

(FRANK steps forward as Royal Commission.)

THOMAS: Hey, would you mind bein' a Royal Commission?

FRANK: Will it take long?

THOMAS: Keep it going a bit, lad, till tempers cool off.

(JACKIE and GEORDIE – as Union and Owners – maintain a tense confrontation as FRANK paces round the floor. One circuit and he returns to THOMAS.)

Well, what hev ye decided?

FRANK: Well, we're against nationalisation?

THOMAS: Good lad. And what about cutting wages?

FRANK: We're against that.

THOMAS: And what about increasing the hours?

FRANK: We're against that.

THOMAS: And what about the coal owners?

FRANK: You can't believe a word they say.

THOMAS: And what about the miners' Union?

FRANK: You can believe every word they say.

THOMAS: Good God, that's even worse.

(Pause.)

Well, that seems like a positive and forward-looking report. Thanks very much.

(Gives him a sugar lump and FRANK retreats into the background.)

JACKIE: But we're no further forward.

GEORDIE: What ye ganna dae, Stanley lad?

THOMAS: That's easy. We'll negotiate.

(Fanfare.)

SLIDE: 1926.

JACKIE: And the world breathed again.

THOMAS: We'll all get together and hammer out a solution.

(THOMAS, JACKIE and GEORDIE — as BALDWIN, the Unions and the Owners — link hands and dance round in a circle, ring-a-roses style. THOMAS breaks free.)

That settles it, the miners'll have to accept a cut in wages.

JACKIE: Will we Hell!

THOMAS: Right, we'll negotiate again.

(They dance round again, till THOMAS breaks off.)

Right, that settles it, the miners will have to accept longer hours.

JACKIE: Will we Hell!

THOMAS: Right we'll negotiate again.

(They dance round again. This time, THOMAS breaks free, but leaves the other two dancing round.)

What they don't know is that it's May 1926 and I'm ready now . . .

(To JACKIE): Did you say something?

JACKIE: I thought we were negotiating . . .

THOMAS: We're doing nothing of the sort. You can all gan on strike and to Hell with the lot of you!

JACKIE: Right, lads, all out.

(Everybody leaves the stage, and the drums roll. A pause and JOHN and RUTH enter, arm in arm.)

JOHN: When we were kids, we didn't have Goldilocks and the three bears like the kids in Jesmond . . . we'd sit on Granda's knee and he'd tell us all about the General Strike . . .

RUTH: No Cinderella?

JOHN: Nae room for Cinderella or her bloody Prince in Brockenback . . . just Arthur Cook and Stanley Baldwin and Will Lawther and Sam Watson and Page Arnot . . .

RUTH: Did you listen to him?

JOHN: Every last word.

RUTH: I've got a friend who's written a thesis about it . . .

JOHN: You don't have to write about it . . . it's built into your brain . . . I mean, I can tell you the story, if you're interested . . .

RUTH: I'm interested . . .

JOHN: Listening?

RUTH: Every last word.

JOHN: Well . . . the first thing to know about the General Strike is that my Granda ran it all himself . . .

RUTH: You mean he was involved in the Strike?

JOHN: Involved? You'd think he's invented it. He was in charge of the pickets in the village.

THOMAS: Right, lads . . . like I said.

(JACKIE and GEORDIE march and counter-march, in a slight parody of the guards outside the Palace, but with strike banners.)

GEORDIE: What we on the look-out for?

THOMAS: Unauthorised vehicles.

GEORDIE: How do we know which one is authorised?

THOMAS: You ask me and I tell you.

GEORDIE: I see.

(GEORDIE points to something off-stage.)

What's that one, then?

JACKIE: Is it an armoured car?

THOMAS: Don't be stupid.

GEORDIE: They reckon the Government sent fourteen armoured cars to protect a milk cart gannin' from Newcastle to South Shields . . .

JACKIE: What happened?

GEORDIE: The horse dropped down dead in Gateshead.

JACKIE: Do you wonder?

VICAR: 'All Our Yesterdays' . . . an everyday story of country folk . . . The General Strike as seen by the newsreel cameras and commentators of the day.

(FRANK does the Pathe News cockerel while the others win Wimbledon, swim the Channel, etc.)

JACKIE: Who says the General Strike's a serious business? They certainly don't think so down here where you're watching a charity football match between a police team and a team of strikers . . .

(The two teams run out.)

And here comes the wife of the Chief Constable to kick off . . .

(MARY forward.)

FRANK: Where's the ball?

GEORDIE: Never mind the ball, let's get on with the game.

(Team carry off MARY.)

JACKIE: And a good time is had by all . . . The result? Oh, the strikers win by two goals to one . . . but who cares about the result, the game's the thing . . . And the hit song of the moment is . . .

EXPERT (sings): 'A room with a view . . .

ALL (off): Hadaway to Hell.

FRANK: Meanwhile the nation marches on with all transport in the hands of voluntary labour. In Newcastle upon Tyne, a train steamed into the central station driven by a driver wearing plus fours — you don't see many of those — and missed the platform. A striker, full of typical Geordie humour shouted . . .

JACKIE: 'divven bother, hinnie, you stay where you are — we'll move the platform.'

FRANK: All over the country people are flocking to the aid of the country . . .

EXPERT: I say, how would you like to flock to the aid of the country?

JACKIE: Why don't you flock yourself?

EXPERT: If you become a special constable we'll give you 46/3 a week, 46/3 a week . . . and a house!

JACKIE: Thinks. If I gan back to the pit I'll only get 31/7¼ a week, and no house.

(JACKIE moves in menacingly.)

EXPERT: You're forgetting something very important.

JACKIE: What?

EXPERT: Everybody's singing . . . 'A room with a view, for two . . .

(JACKIE chases him off-stage.)

FRANK (Commentator): But it isn't all singing at this time of crisis in the land. The Armed Forces are on the alert.

(The lads are lined up like an Army squad with SERGEANT reading out Churchill's directive.)

SERGEANT (Geordie): Now then, lads . . here's a message specially for you from the Home Secretary . . .

SOLDIER (Jackie): Winston S . . . ?

GEORDIE: That's the one . . . any action you horrible lot have to take to aid the Civil Power will receive the full support of His Majesty's Government . . .

(Pause.)

Step forward any man that doesn't understand what that means.

(ALL step forward.)

You horrible lot. What he means is, if you see any strikers causing trouble, it's shoot first and no questions afterwards. Yes, what's the matter with you?

JACKIE: Well, my father and two brothers is on strike. Supposing . . .

GEORDIE: Oh, you needn't shoot them, just hit them with your rifle butt.

JACKIE: Oh, righto.

GEORDIE: By the left . . . 'A room with a view' . . .

(They march off, singing in chorus.)

VICAR: And so throughout the length and breadth of the land people are girding their loins for the struggle to come, urged on by the inspiring words of Rudyard Kipling . . .

FRANK:
Keep ye the law — be swift in all obedience,
Clear the land of evil, drive the road and bridge the ford,
Make ye sure to each his own,
That ye reap what he hath sown,
By the peace among our people, let men know we serve the Lord.

JACKIE: Just a minute . . .

FRANK: I beg your pardon . . .

JACKIE: We've got poets on wor side an' all . . .

FRANK: Just a moment . . .

JACKIE: Hadaway to Hell.

(Pushes FRANK away.)

We have fed you all for a hundred years
But that was our doom, you know.
From the time you chained us in the fields
To the strike a week ago
You have eaten our lives, our babies, our wives,
But that was our legal share
But if blood be the price of our legal wealth,
Good God we have bought it fair.

(Cheers and counter cheers.)

COMMENTATOR: Meanwhile the whole world was singing . . . 'A room with a view'.

VICAR: Wrong, my child.

EXPERT: I do beg your pardon, bishop.

VICAR: I'll tell you what the world is singing. (Sings.)
Not a penny off the pay
Not a minute on the day.

ALL: Amen.

VICAR:
Blessed are the coal owners who make such fair demands.
Blessed are the blacklegs who come from foreign lands.
Blessed are the constables with truncheons in their hands.

And the voice of the miners was heard and the porridge of the nation . . .

GEORDIE: . . . was stirred.

THOMAS: I, Stanley Baldwin, have an important announcement to make . . .

(A hush.)

I, Stanley Baldwin, have resumed negotiations with the TUC. I, Stanley Baldwin, have brought the General Strike to an end, thus preserving democratic government, the Monarchy, the strength of sterling, the Marylebone Cricket Club and I, Stanley Baldwin . . .

GEORDIE: Goodness me, Stanley, you must be the greatest Prime Minister that ever lived.

THOMAS: I think I must be.

GEORDIE: Altogether now . . .

ALL (exeunt singing): 'A room with a view . . . '

(Back at the party again.)

THOMAS: May 14th the General Strike ended . . . but the miners stayed out till the October . . .

MARY: Gluttons for punishment.

THOMAS: Men.

MARY: Who's talking about the men?

JACKIE: I tell my kids how me and me brothers and sisters stayed alive, 'cause of the soup kitchens and they think I'm jokin' . . . didn't keep my mother alive, though.

THOMAS: We shouldn't have gone back in the October either.

GEORDIE: Fellers started to gan back, didn't they?

THOMAS: Not in Durham they didn't . . . solid as a rock . . . Nottingham-shire and Derbyshire they went back . . . the bastards . . . and they near wrecked the Union . . .

FRANK: Did you win the strike?

THOMAS: They reduced the wages.

VICAR: You lost?

THOMAS: The miners never won a strike yet . . . not till years later . . .

MARY: They didn't reduce your wages.

THOMAS: No.

VICAR: How was that?

MARY: No job, no wages.

THOMAS: I was a lodge official, you see . . .

FRANK: I thought there was no victimisation . . .

JACKIE: Thirty-five thousand miners didn't get their jobs back in this country . . . that's a lot of victimisation.

GEORDIE: Mind you, it was all in the national interest.

JACKIE: Oh, aye, it makes you feel a lot warmer inside.

FRANK: Why is it?

(Pause.)

THOMAS: 'Cause it's the same fellers, that's why . . .

JACKIE: In 1832 . . .

THOMAS: Lords and landowners . . .

JACKIE: In 1926 . . .

THOMAS: Lords and landowners . . .

JACKIE: In 1968.

THOMAS: The Stock Exchange . . .

GEORDIE: Lords and landowners . . .

FRANK: They don't own the coalmines . . .

GEORDIE: They've got the banks and the jockey club, that's enough . . . never mind, comes the revolution . . .

JACKIE: That'll make all the difference.

(Music starts. GEORDIE steps forward for his song. Everybody joins in the chorus.)

GEORDIE (sings):

I should have done it yesterday
If I hadn't had a cold
But since I've put this pint away,
I've never felt so bold.

ALL:

So as soon as this pub closes,
As soon as this pub closes,
As soon as this pub closes,
The revolution starts.

GEORDIE:

I'll shoot the aristocracy
And confiscate their brass
Create a fine democracy
That's truly working class.

ALL:

As soon as this pub closes,
As soon as this pub closes,
As soon as this pub closes,
We'll raise the banner high.

GEORDIE:

I'll fight the nasty racialists
And scrap the colour bar
Old Enoch and his followers
And every commissar.

ALL:

As soon as this pub closes,
As soon as this pub closes,
As soon as this pub closes,
We'll man the barricades.

GEORDIE:

So raise your glasses, everyone
For everything is planned
And each and every mother's son
Will see the promised land.

ALL:

So as soon as this pub closes,
As soon as this pub closes,
As soon as this pub closes . . .

GEORDIE (speaks): I think I'm goin' to be sick . . .

(He makes a dash for it.)

ALL:

The revolution comes.

(Into a big, noisy, singing, dancing finish, and a cross-fade to JOHN and RUTH. Very quiet.)

RUTH: Why do you bother?

JOHN: What do you mean?

RUTH: Digging coal . . . if it's just been a hundred and fifty years of oppression?

JOHN: Do you really want to know?

RUTH: Every last word, John.

JOHN: 'Cause I don't know any better . . . a hundred years, and I don't know any better . . . I'm like that bloody slag-heap . . . built into the landscape . . . just as solid, just as thick . . .

RUTH: Sad, isn't it?

JOHN: I don't think about it much — it's only people like you makes us think about it.

RUTH: Why not leave?

JOHN: Leave?

RUTH: Leave the pit . . . leave the village? . . . You're a big strong man.

JOHN: I could get a job at my trade on Teesside, I daresay . . . engineering, you know if I fancied it . . .

RUTH: So when are you going?

JOHN: You're not very bright, are you, for a scholar?

RUTH: Thanks very much . . .

JOHN: Nae good being upset about it, you're not . . . There's two old folk in there need someone to look after them like they looked after me . . .

RUTH: I'm talking about now . . . your grandparents are part of the past . . .

JOHN: It's all they've got, isn't it?

RUTH: Yes, but you can't live in the past . . . the General Strike was forty years ago . . .

JOHN: It didn't stop with the General Strike − that was just the beginning.

(Into Thirties sequence.)

THOMAS: 1931.

(March to form a queue.)

1931, Ramsay Macdonald.

GEORDIE: Jeanette Macdonald.

JACKIE: Donald Duck.

GEORDIE: Mickey Mouse.

JACKIE: Pluto.

THOMAS: Back to Ramsay Macdonald. Well, lads, what are we ganna dae about this?

JACKIE: Only one thing for it.

GEORDIE: Howay, let's march on Whitehall.

(They unfurl 'WE WANT WORK' banner − the band strikes up, they march off and on stage again.)

He seemed a canny enough fellow that Deputy Assistant Parliamentary Private Secretary.

THOMAS: He didn't dae nothing.

GEORDIE: Ah . . . but the conscience of the nation was stirred.

(Cross-fade to JOHN and RUTH.)

RUTH: The trouble is, you . . . all, of you, sit around the village, sorry for yourself because you think nobody cares . . .

JOHN: You reckon someone does care?

RUTH: Of course they do.

JOHN: Name one.

RUTH: I care.

JOHN: What you ganna dae? Start a soup kitchen?

RUTH: That's not what I mean, John. What happens when your grandparents . . . I mean, they're getting on a bit and . . .

JOHN: When they die, you mean?

RUTH: Yes.

JOHN: I mean, we just say it — we live with it round here.

RUTH: Would you leave then?

JOHN: I told you.

RUTH: Supposing you met a girl you fancied?

JOHN: Getaway.

RUTH: It can happen . . .

JOHN: I've never been fancied by a scholar before . . .

RUTH: Don't expect too much . . .

(They kiss.)

JOHN: Well, that'll dae. For a down payment.

(Cross-fade to the queue.)

THOMAS: 1934. Stanley Baldwin.

JACKIE: Oh, not him again!

THOMAS: Sorry, lads . . . Stanley Baldwin.

JACKIE: Ye bugger, he's a sticker, I'll say that for him.

THOMAS: Stanley Baldwin.

GEORDIE: Stanley Matthews.

JACKIE: Jessie Matthews.

THOMAS: Mickey Mouse.

JACKIE: Pluto.

GEORDIE: Donald Duck.

THOMAS: Stanley Baldwin. Howay, lads.

(Marching procedure as before.)

JACKIE: Pity he couldn't see us personally.

GEORDIE: He seemed canny enough, that office boy . . .

JACKIE: Oh, aye.

THOMAS: Nothing's happened . . . everything's still the same.

GEORDIE: But Tommy lad, we stirred the conscience of the nation.

(Cross-fade to JOHN and RUTH.)

JOHN: Bonny, isn't it?

RUTH: Slag-heap by moonlight.

JOHN: Aye. They reckon the NCB's ganna plant grass on that one day and call it part of wor island heritage.

RUTH: They'll maybe do the same for you.

JOHN: With me they call it redundancy payments. Grass — they could cover it with icing sugar — it wouldn't alter the fact that underneath it's all waste.

RUTH: It's sort of beautiful . . .

JOHN: I've noticed that sometimes . . . when I've had a few pints . . .

RUTH: You're sober now.

JOHN: I know, that's why it worries me, I'm thinking it's maybe something to do with you . . . Howay, I'll give you a conducted tour of the slag-heap.

RUTH: Now?

JOHN: It's where all the courting couples go round here . . . and a pitman's woman does as she's told . . .

RUTH: Who says I'm a pitman's woman?

JOHN: Up to you, bonny lass — those are the terms. I'll show you the slag-heap.

RUTH: The waste.

JOHN: It's all waste around here — nothing else to look at. Come on, I'll show you.

(*They go off. Cross-fade to the queue as before.*)

SLIDE: 1937.

THOMAS: 1937. Neville Chamberlain.

JACKIE: God help us.

GEORDIE: Wee Ellen Wilkinson.

THOMAS: Hughie Gallagher.

JACKIE: Willie Gallagher.

GEORDIE: Patsy Gallagher and Raich Carter and Sunderland won the Cup.

JACKIE: Long time ago.

GEORDIE: Donald Duck, Mickey Mouse and Pluto . . .

THOMAS: And Neville Chamberlain.

(*Pause.*)

Howay, lads.

(*And off they go with the banner again, as before. Off-stage, then on again but this time they are joined by FRANK, dressed as a very slick 1969 lad — say a young chap from a shipyard dressed for a night out* in Newcastle.)

Well.

JACKIE: Well, I hope that office cleaner passes the message on, that's all . . .

GEORDIE: Never mind, lads, the conscience of . . . you know, I think the nation's forgettin' an' all . . .

(They are uneasily aware of FRANK's presence.)

THOMAS: Is he with you?

JACKIE: No.

GEORDIE: Never seen him before.

THOMAS: Try an experiment. Right?

(They nod.)

Neville Chamberlain.

JACKIE: Ellen Wilkinson.

GEORDIE: Hughie Gallagher.

FRANK: Englebert Humperdinck.

(They stare at FRANK, shattered. Music starts and FRANK moves forward for his song.)

FRANK (sings):
When me father was a lad
Unemployment was so bad
He spent best part of his life down at the dole.
Straight from school to the labour queue
Raggy clothes and holey shoes
Combin' pit-heaps for a manky bag o' coal.
And I'm standin' at the door, at the same old bloody door,
Waiting for the pay-out as me father did before.

Nowadays we've got a craze
To follow clever Keynsian ways
And computers measure economic growth.
We've got experts milling round
Writing theories on the pound
Caring little whether we can buy a loaf.
And I'm standin' at the door, at the same old bloody door,
Waiting for the pay-out like me father did before.

'Course we didn't like the freeze
But we really tried to please
'Cause we made that little cross to put them in.
Down the river we've been sold
For a pot of cheap Swiss gold
And we're the ones that suffer for their sin.
And I'm standin' at the door, at the same old bloody door,

Waiting for the pay-out as me father did before.

Baby, baby, this is true,
I'll be standin' in this queue,
Till the Tyne runs clear and plastic roses sing.
So the next time they come by,
Watch the sky for the custard pie,
And tell 'em straight, it's Humperdinck for King!
And I'm standin' at the door, at the same old bloody door,
Waiting for the pay-out like me father did before.

(FRANK leads everybody back into the party, the house, and the present, with an all-join-in chorus finish and applause out of which THOMAS speaks.)

THOMAS: Good lad, Frank . . . I never knew you had it in you . . .

FRANK: I'm not just a pretty face, you know . . .

THOMAS: No, I enjoyed that . . .

MARY: I always told you he was a good lad . . . all we can get out of you is pitman John . . .

FRANK: Where is John, anyway?

JACKIE: He'll be down the yard.

THOMAS: And your Ruth?

GEORDIE: Is it a two-seater netty you've got, Tommy?

(And the truth dawns on FRANK, as they look at him, expectantly. He goes to the door and outside. JOHN and RUTH in the middle of a warm, rather than passionate, embrace — but enough implications to satisfy all tastes. Everybody sees the confrontation.)

THOMAS: Well, I know the right and proper thing to do.

MARY: Shuttup, man . . .

FRANK: Well, let's do the right and proper thing, eh . . . ?

(FRANK takes off his jacket.)

JOHN: No.

FRANK: We've got to maintain the old traditions.

JOHN: Don't be daft, man.

FRANK: How do you know I wouldn't enjoy it?

(Pause.)

Scared?

RUTH: Frank, don't be stupid . . .

FRANK: My business, my brother . . .

JOHN: Suit yourself.

(JOHN strips off for the fight.)

THOMAS: I haven't seen a good fight for ages.

MARY: You fool!

RUTH (to MARY): Can't you stop them?

MARY: No, hinny, I can't stop them.

(RUTH looks away.)

No, you've got to watch, pet, that's what it's about.

(They start the fight. In form and action, it is a repeat of the fight in ACT ONE, but a deeper sense of reality. JOHN is bigger, but FRANK has built-in resentment.)

THOMAS: What'll you give us on John?

GEORDIE: You're kidding, Tommy.

THOMAS: Gan on, call yourself a sportsman?

GEORDIE: Four to one on, then.

THOMAS: Go and loss yourself.

(FRANK forces JOHN down, but more of a slip.)

There y'are, it's an even match.

GEORDIE: John's stronger.

JACKIE: Frank's doing very canny.

THOMAS: Aye, but it's not strength, it's jealousy.

VICAR: Stay down, Frank.

THOMAS: Still not giving us a price?

GEORDIE: I'll give you ten to one Frank.

JACKIE: Ye deserve to burn in Hell.

GEORDIE: I'll dae that anyways.

(FRANK goes down, hurt, and stays down.)

THOMAS: Aye, that's the way I read the fight.

MARY: That's all you care? Your grandsons fighting like . . .

THOMAS: Like a couple of pitmen . . . gan on, say it . . .

MARY: Well, pet, you've got to choose, the one on the floor, or the one on his feet . . . Ye bugs, fancy picking the loser.

(As RUTH goes to FRANK, the EXPERT comes on.)

EXPERT: 1939.

THOMAS: 1939. Neville Chamberlain.

GEORDIE: Mickey Mouse.

JACKIE: Pluto.

THOMAS: Neville Chamberlain.

EXPERT: No, no, no . . . Adolf Hitler . . . Come along, chaps, seats in all parts.

(The men line up and go off, like sheep.)

(As HITLER): There will now be an intermission, during which we will fight the Second World War. I therefore order you to take a twelve-minute interval! Sieg Heil!

ACT THREE

A crashing ecclesiastical chord on an organ and dramatic quasi-religious light on the VICAR in pulpit pose.

VICAR: And it came to pass that in the one thousand, nine hundred and forty-seventh year of our Lord, all the earth of the county of Durham did pass into the ownership of the tribes thereof. And the richness of the land did comprise collieries, numbering one hundred and thirty-five, coking plants, numbering sixteen, power stations, numbering eight, brickworks, numbering seventeen, tribal dwellings, numbering twenty-six thousand, fields and vineyards numbering ninety-three thousand acres, and fish and chip shops, numbering one only. And there was weeping and wailing among the rich merchants and moneylenders of the Southern lands, but among the tribes of the North there was great rejoicing. Verily, I say unto you, blessed are the meek, that they shall inherit the earth, and the manifold riches therein.

(Cross-fade to GEORDIE and JACKIE, front of stage, proudly looking at the pithead.)

SLIDE: 1947.

JACKIE: Well, Geordie, tomorrow it all belongs to us.

GEORDIE: I never thought to see the day of nationalisation.

JACKIE: A Labour Government that believes in Socialism.

GEORDIE: At last, we're ganna taste the fruits of wor labours.

(Into their song and dance routine.)

When it's ours, Jackie boy, when it's ours,
There'll be changes, bonny lad, when it's ours.
When us colliers take control,
No more twelve-inch seams of coal,
No more means-test, no more dole,
When it's ours, all ours.

GEORDIE (speaks): I saw Manny Shinwell lookin' at Seaham Colliery, saying . . . 'Mine, all mine . . .'

When it's ours, Geordie lad, when it's ours,
Man, what glorious times we'll have when it's ours,
What's the future hold for me?
You can retire at twenty-three!
On full pension? Nat'rally!
When it's ours, all ours.

GEORDIE (speaks): So I gans on holiday to the South of France and I say to the waiter, 'Hev ye got frogs legs?' . . . 'Mais oui, hinny,' he says . . .

'Right,' I says 'Hop off and fetch us some nice pease pudding.'

When it's ours, Jackie boy, when it's ours,
I've got plans, bonny lad, when it's ours,
Bye, we'll really live it up,
Only best champagne we'll sup,
While Newcastle win the Cup,
When it's ours, all ours.

JACKIE (speaks): Did you gan to see Newcastle play on Saturday?

GEORDIE: No . . . well, they didn't come to see me when I was bad.

When it's ours, Geordie lad, when it's ours,
Mind the wife'll be reet glad when it's ours,
Tell me Jackie, what's in store,
What will she be grateful for?
Why, I'll stop in bed wi' her,
When it's ours, all ours.

GEORDIE (speaks): So I says to the gaffer, 'Can I hev the day off work,
my wife's expecting a baby' . . . 'Certainly' he says 'when's the baby
due?' I says 'Nine months time'.

When it's ours Jackie boy, when it's ours,
We'll be masters, bonny lad, when it's ours,
(Ultra posh): We may step lightly on the grass
To let Lord Londonderry pass
Then we'll kick him up the path,
When it's ours, all ours.

GEORDIE (speaks): So Lord Londonderry had this dream. He dreamed he
was making an important speech in the House of Lord and when he woke
up, he was . . .

When it's ours, Geordie lad, when it's ours,
There'll be changes, bonny lad, when it's ours,
(Doubtful): Are ye sure we'll be all right?
Is the future *really* bright?

JACKIE (speaks): Oh, for God's sake, man, Geordie . . .

We *won* this bloody fight,
So it's ours, all ours.

When it's ours, Jackie boy, when it's ours,
Oh what holidays we'll have, when it's ours,
California, Santa Fe,
Winter sports and Saint Tropez,
And to Hell with Whitley Bay!
When it's ours, all ours.

(A big finish and music-hall exit. Fading up lights on the house as JOHN
is getting ready to go on night shift.)

JOHN: Good night, Grandma . . .

MARY: Good night, son.

JOHN: Good night, Granda . . .

THOMAS: Safe home, lad.

JOHN: Good night. (General.)

> (They all wish JOHN good night. He goes outside with FRANK and RUTH.)

> Good night, kiddar.

FRANK: Good night.

JOHN: Sorry if I hurt ye . . .

FRANK: It didn't hurt a bit.

> (But his eye is black for all that.)

JOHN: Oh what a pity, thank God.

> (Pause.)

> Good night, I said.

FRANK: Just waiting for . . .

> (Meaning RUTH.)

JOHN: I'll send her in the house after.

> (Pausc.)

> Gan on . . . or I'll close the other eye.

> (FRANK goes in.)

RUTH: You're a big man, aren't you?

JOHN: Ye have to be.

RUTH: Did you want to be alone?

JOHN: Questions to ask . . .

RUTH: Like?

JOHN: Like why did you pick him up when he was lying on the floor?

RUTH: It's the way I'm brought up . . . somebody gets knocked over, I just go and help him to his feet.

JOHN: Even if he's the loser?

RUTH: You're the loser, big man.

JOHN: How come?

RUTH: You're the one that's flat on your back . . . like everybody in the village . . . and you won't let anybody help you up . . .

JOHN: Not if it means leaving, no . . .

RUTH: You stay here . . . and you'd expect me to come running . . .

JOHN: It's a pit village . . . you snap your fingers, the womenfolk do come running . . .

RUTH: Scrubbing the back . . .

JOHN: Aye, and tending the wounds.

RUTH: It's not a pit village. It's a ghost village. No call for pitmen any more . . . no call for their womenfolk.

JOHN: Somebody's still got to dig the coal somewhere.

RUTH: I wouldn't come here . . . or anywhere else . . . not for a pitman.

JOHN: Too proud, is it?

RUTH: Too cowardly.

(Pause.)

JOHN: Makes sense. You'll be here when I get back.

RUTH: Are you asking me or telling me?

JOHN: I'm telling you.

RUTH: Snapping your fingers.

JOHN: You spend half your life underground. There's no time for debates when you're on the surface.

RUTH: And the rest of the world move over . . .

JOHN: That's right. You try digging coal for a hundred and fifty years . . . see what it does to you . . .

RUTH: For a man that isn't interested in the history of the workers, you've got a lot to say about it . . .

JOHN: I'm not interested in who built the prison walls or what sort of bricks they used . . . but I know the walls are there just the same . . .

RUTH: It's not a prison. You've got the key.

JOHN: Lost the key years ago . . . hole in my pocket.

RUTH: You want to leave the pit, don't you?

(Pause.)

JOHN: We all do, if we're honest . . . we don't talk about it . . . but we all want to leave . . . but you've made me say it out loud . . . I'm not sure I can forgive you for that.

RUTH: I'll be here when you get back.

(JOHN moves away.)

JOHN: Do you know what a pitman's woman does when her man gans off to work?

RUTH: What?

JOHN: She watches him go, just in case.

RUTH: I'm not a pitman's woman.

JOHN: You're very wise, bonny lass.

(He goes, and she watches him. Silence. Then the bell rings, a harsh intrusion. THOMAS comes out of the house quickly and sets the winding gear in motion. The cage comes up to the surface — all as at the beginning of ACT ONE — and WILL JOBLING comes out of the cage.)

THOMAS: Howay, Will, man, I thought you'd forgotten . . .

WILL: I just love my work, man, cannot drag myself away.

THOMAS: Double or quits again?

WILL: Gan on.

(THOMAS tosses the coins. They watch them fall. THOMAS is the winner.)

THOMAS: Hard luck, Will . . . it's the following wind.

WILL: Ye bugger.

(He pays up. MARY comes out.)

MARY: Howay in, you two, I know what you're up to.

WILL: Just safeguarding the future of the Coal Board, hinny, that's all . . .

MARY: Aye, I know . . .

GEORDIE (to the audience): Oh, she's a lovely woman, my wife, she can be an angel . . . and the sooner the better.

(MARY, THOMAS and WILL go into the house. RUTH is also in the house now.)

JACKIE: Them pumps in good order, Will lad?

WILL: Oh, aye, they'll look after theirselves for a while . . .

GEORDIE: How long?

WILL: Two or three pints, I daresay.

VICAR: There you are, Mr Jobling.

(He gives WILL a drink. The VICAR is acting as barman.)

WILL: Ta. Here's to the two of you . . . (Thomas and Mary.)

THOMAS: Thanks, lad.

MARY: Thanks, William.

THOMAS: Hey, listen to that . . . William, indeed . . .

WILL: Been having a good crack, hev ye?

VICAR: I've just been learning about nationalisation, Mr Jobling . . .

WILL: Oh, divven talk to me about nationalisation . . .

MARY: Ye'll never stop him, now . . .

WILL: Nationalisation! (Outrage.)

JACKIE: What's the matter with it, man? The workers must take over the means of production . . .

WILL: Utopia, they telled me, bloody Utopia, and I comes in, first day at work after nationalisation . . . and what do I see?

THOMAS: I've heard it all before.

WILL: What do I see?

GEORDIE: We're bursting to find out . . .

WILL: The same gaffers.

(Pause.)

JACKIE: Don't be daft, man . . .

WILL: The same gaffers, I'm telling ye, there's Alfie Robson standin' there, same as he had done for twenty-odd years . . . five foot nowt and nasty with it.

JACKIE: Alfie Robson didn't own the pit, he was only the manager . . . he wasn't the owner . . .

WILL: Who's talking about owners? I'm talking about gaffers.

THOMAS: You're talking a lot of bloody rubbish, I'll say that.

JACKIE: And I'll tell you something an' all . . . there's no better record of labour relations anywhere than in the Durham coalfield since nationalisation . . . twenty years and not one official strike . . . not one . . .

WILL: And that's another thing.

MARY: I thought it might be.

WILL: Nae decent strikes any more.

JACKIE: That's good, isn't it, nobody really wants strikes.

WILL: There's nae fun any more.

THOMAS: Take no notice of the old fool.

WILL: And that's not the worst of it . . .

(WILL is just getting warmed up.)

THOMAS: Hey, Will, man, get in yon cage and hadaway inbye, I'm sick of ye.

WILL: I haven't finished yet.

GEORDIE: Well, hurry up and finish . . .

WILL: What about rationalisation?

(Pause.)

JACKIE: Rationalisation?

WILL: Aye.

JACKIE: Nobody's talking about rationalisation . . .

WILL: I'm talking about it.

THOMAS: The subject on the agenda is nationalisation.

WILL: Bust the agenda, I'm talking about rationalisation.

MARY: I don't know what anybody's talking about.

RUTH: Me neither.

THOMAS: It's nowt to do with women.

FRANK: What about rationalisation?

WILL: And you a scholar . . .

FRANK: I'm sorry, I don't see the connection . . .

WILL: The connection is that this village, and this pit, got rationalisation.

(Pause.)

JACKIE: Aye.

GEORDIE: That's right.

THOMAS: I know.

VICAR: How do you mean? The pit got rationalisation?

WILL: I mean, the NCB says we've got to rationalise the industry . . . we've got to rationalise Brockenback pit . . .

(Pause.)

I mean, they closed the bugger.

(Music link, a lighting change and the Labour Exchange door is pushed on again. THOMAS, WILL, JACKIE and GEORDIE form a queue.)

SLIDE: 1961.

THOMAS: 1961. Harold Macmillan.

JACKIE: Selwyn Lloyd.

WILL: Huckleberry Hound.

GEORDIE: Yogi Bear.

THOMAS: Harold Macmillan.

(Pause.)

We're here again, lads.

WILL: This is what they mean by rationalisation.

JACKIE: Marginal adjustments in the national economy.

GEORDIE: Safeguarding the strength of sterling.

JACKIE: Our world role.

WILL: Wor seat at the conference table.

THOMAS: Well, it still feels like the dole to me.

JACKIE: Only one thing to do.

WILL: Whitehall it'll have to be.

(Marching music building up quietly.)

GEORDIE: We'll have to stir the conscience of the nation.

(The old banners are brought out.)

THOMAS: Are you ready, lads?

(The music building up.)

By the left . . . quick march . . .

(Just as they are about to set off, the EXPERT comes on from the opposite side. He is dressed as a high Cabinet man, and carries a brief case.)

EXPERT: Don't you go to all that trouble, chaps, we'll come to you.

(And he crosses to them. They are stunned.)

THOMAS: Ye what?

EXPERT: I am coming to you.

THOMAS: Wey, that's a turn-up.

EXPERT: Well, you see, I'm on a fact-finding mission.

JACKIE: What sort of facts do you expect to find?

EXPERT: One can't really say that, till one has, as it were, found them.

(He roots around the stage looking for facts.)

The point is, gentlemen . . . chaps . . . lads . . . we are very worried about the results of nationalisation and, er . . . rationalisation, in this area . . .

THOMAS: So are we!

JACKIE: What are ye ganna dae about it?

EXPERT: We have perfected a new policy . . . regionalisation!

(Fanfare.)

THOMAS: Regionalisation?

WILL: Getaway.

JACKIE: That sounds grand.

GEORDIE: But what is it?

EXPERT: It simply means that from now on, we in Whitehall are determined to take a fresh look at your splendid chaps, lads in Durham and Northumberland and . . . Yorkshire's quite near as well, isn't it?

JACKIE: You mean we'll get a bigger slice of the national cake.

EXPERT: Yes . . . and very nicely put, if I may say so.

JACKIE: Ta.

THOMAS: But you're all Tories, aren't you?

EXPERT: Well lads, we're all Tories now, unless we're Socialists . . .

WILL: That's true enough.

EXPERT: My friends . . .

THOMAS: Watch him . . .

EXPERT: My friends . . . we're all brothers in the same family . . .

THOMAS: Prove it!

EXPERT: I can prove it, friends . . . because I have brought with me on my fact-finding mission our new secret weapon. Our new symbol of liberty, equality and fraternity.

(As the music starts he brings out of his brief case a cloth cap, two sizes too large . . . and sings . . .)

SLIDES: HAILSHAM, HOME, MACMILLAN, GEORGE BROWN in caps.

If you ever go to Tyneside you must watch your P's and Q's,
You must learn to say 'Newcassel' or their confidence you'll lose.
And in mingling with the common folk you're sure to make a botch,
If you ask for pints of bitter, what you really mean is Scotch.

But there's one thing makes the locals really fall into your lap
Get your picture in the papers with a little cloth cap,
A little cloth cap, a little cloth cap,
You'll make a big impression with a little cloth cap.

You must use the local language when you're talking to the men,
Say a miner is a 'pitman' and they'll ask you back again.
And remember when you're in the pub to spit upon the floor,
And if you chew tobacco, well, the compliments will pour.

But there's one thing makes the locals really fall into your lap,
Get your picture in the papers with a little cloth cap;
A little cloth cap, a little cloth cap,
You can eat your singing hinnies from your little cloth cap.

(He makes the song a triumphal procession ending with a big flourishing exit. The men are left feeling quite pleased until they realise they are still standing at the Labour Exchange door.)

THOMAS: Well, it's all very well but I divven feel any different.

(The VICAR walks across to them.)

VICAR: I hear they're closing the pit.

THOMAS: That's right.

VICAR: Perhaps I could say a few suitable words . . .

GEORDIE: We've already said a few suitable words . . .

WILL: And it's staying closed.

VICAR: Well, haven't they made any arrangements?

THOMAS: Oh, aye, they're looking after us . . . me and Will here, we're ganna look after the pumps . . .

JACKIE: And me and Geordie, we're ganna be redeployed to Datton Colliery . . . temporarily . . .

VICAR: Temporarily?

JACKIE: Till they build the perfume factory.

VICAR: They're going to build a perfume factory here?

GEORDIE: To take up the slack of unemployment . . .

JACKIE: They're not actually building it yet . . . they're doing a feasibility study . . . to see whether it's the right place for a perfume factory.

THOMAS: There's got to be an adequate water supply before you can build a perfume factory.

WILL: And proper sewage disposal.

GEORDIE: And the right kind of prevailing winds.

JACKIE: You can't just bash a perfume factory down anywhere.

GEORDIE: Diversification.

WILL: What?

GEORDIE: Diversification . . . that's what they call it when they close a pit and build a perfume factory . . .

WILL: Look, for God's sake, Geordie man, we've had nationalisation and rationalisation . . . and then regionalisation . . . and now diversification . . . I divven think I can take any more . . .

GEORDIE: All we lack's constipation.

JACKIE: I've got news for you.

GEORDIE: Oh, I'm sorry . . . keep taking the tablets . . .

(FRANK suddenly leaps up from his place in the house, very triumphant.)

FRANK: There's something you're all forgetting.

THOMAS: What's that.

FRANK: The wind of change.

GEORDIE: Stop taking the tablets.

WILL: Back to the perfume factory again.

FRANK: No, not that at all.

THOMAS: What's he talking about?

FRANK: An eleven per cent swing in Gosforth, that's what I'm talking about.

(A loud fanfare.)

1964.

SLIDE: 1964.

Labour elected!

(Fanfare.)

(During the following sequence, the characters assume positions as follows: GEORDIE, FRANK and RUTH as the three candidates, JACKIE as the chairman of television panel consisting of THOMAS, MARY and the VICAR, and WILL as the swing expert. Very casual and accidental-looking, slipping back into a party atmosphere at the end without any formal link.)

JACKIE: Here is the result for Jesmond Dene South.

GEORDIE: Harry Bradley, Labour, 26,973 . . .

FRANK: Ernest Gordon-hyphen-Bennett, Conservative, 7574 . . .

RUTH: Janie Potbender, Liberal, 3886 . . .

JACKIE: Labour elected . . . after a recount . . .

GEORDIE: And I would like to thank my opponents . . .

FRANK: My constituency workers without whom . . .

RUTH: And the Official Receiver, I mean Returning Officer, for . . .

GEORDIE: A good . . .

FRANK: Clean . . .

RUTH: Fight . . .

JACKIE: And now for their comments on that result from Jesmond Dene South . . . ·

THOMAS: They're all a set of villains, I don't know why you're getting so excited . . .

MARY: I'm sorry the little Liberal lass lost her deposit, she's a bonny lass . . .

THOMAS: I bet she lost more than her deposit . . .

MARY: That'll do, Thomas Milburn . . .

VICAR: The glory is not in the winning but in the taking part.

JACKIE: And for a comment on the swing . . .

WILL: Well, according to my slide rule and my piece of string, if that swing is repeated throughout the country, Labour will have an overall majority of 769.

JACKIE: Wey, you daft devil, there's only just over six hundred seats altogether . . .

WILL: Well it's an old bit of string, man, Jackie . . .

JACKIE: And that's a very old joke.

FRANK: It's a great victory, though.

GEORDIE: It certainly is.

JACKIE: Our movement.

(And now we're in an election celebration party.)

GEORDIE: Aye.

JACKIE: The Labour movement that was made by the miners out of blood, sweat and tears . . .

ALL: That's right, hear hear . . .

JACKIE: The men we've stood and cheered as they've spoken from the platform at the miners gala in Durham . . .

FRANK: A great victory.

GEORDIE: Brothers, we're on our way . . .

JACKIE: The Labour movement . . .

(They raise their glasses in a toast. THOMAS hesitates.)

What's the matter, Tommy?

THOMAS: You'll not remember Ramsay MacDonald . . .

JACKIE: Never mind ancient history, man . . . I'm giving you a toast . . . the Labour movement . . .

(They drink the toast. Glasses down and there is a knock at the door. THOMAS opens the door. There stands the EXPERT, smartly dressed in a Harold Wilson mac.)

EXPERT: I wonder if I might join the party, brothers . . .

THOMAS: Certainly, come along in . . .

EXPERT: Thanks, brothers . . .

(He joins them. A glass is thrust into his hands. He drinks with careful robustness.)

JACKIE: I don't think we've met, have we?

EXPERT: No, I don't think so . . . I don't get up this way all that often . . .

THOMAS: The face is familiar.

EXPERT: Well . . . you could say I am a close personal friend of Mrs Barbara Castle, to name but a few . . . perhaps if we say a Government spokesman . . .

THOMAS: But a loyal member of the Movement?

EXPERT: Goodness, yes, when the Whips are out I'll vote for anything . . .

GEORDIE: And what was it you wanted?

EXPERT: Well, I've just popped in to explain the Government's fuel policy . . .

MARY: That's very civil . . . have a seat, pet.

WILL: Just hold hard a minute, brother . . . is it to do with nationalisation?

EXPERT: Partly, yes.

FRANK: Rationalisation?

EXPERT: That comes into it.

RUTH: Regionalisation?

EXPERT: Oh yes, I'm a firm believer in regionalisation . . . the Development Councils and Dan Smith and touring outlying areas with popular selections from Marat-Sade. I believe in all of that.

JACKIE: How about . . . diversification?

EXPERT: I'm glad you asked me that . . . expecially diversification.

JACKIE: Like perfume factories . . .

EXPERT: Given my own way, perfume factories will spring up like daffodils in March . . . which brings me to my fuel policy . . .

THOMAS: Go on.

EXPERT: Anybody heard of nuclear reactors?

GEORDIE: Aye, they dropped one on Hartlepools, just missed the monkey.

EXPERT: Oh no, these are good things, definitely good things.

VICAR: I take it you're bringing tidings of great joy . . . ?

EXPERT: Unquestionably brother, er, father . . . but not in so many words . . .

FRANK: Nuclear reactors you were talking about.

EXPERT: And . . .

(Pause.)

High . . . speed . . . gas . . .

(He kneels.)

ALL: High speed gas?

(The EXPERT gets up.)

JACKIE: Well, we know all about gas, you make it out of coal. Like electricity, you make that out of coal an' all.

EXPERT: How many of you know the North Sea?

JACKIE: The North Sea. Aye, ye can just see it from Whitley Bay . . .

EXPERT: And what lies beneath the North Sea, full forty fathoms deep?

(Pause.)

GEORDIE: Bird's Eye cod pieces?

EXPERT: High speed gas.

(A quick kneel.)

Which we shall suck up from the sea-bed in great man-made vacuum cleaners and then blow it out over this green and pleasant land as the basis of the technological revolution.

JACKIE: Natural gas.

EXPERT: High speed ... natural gas ... as you so well put it. Armed only with nuclear reactors and high speed gas the nation shall scale the heights ...

THOMAS: And what happens to coal?

(Pause.)

EXPERT: What ... happens ... to ... coal.

THOMAS: Aye.

EXPERT: I'm glad you asked me that.

THOMAS: Let's hev an answer, then.

EXPERT: Well, we have a programme in mind ... based on a carefully considered ... de-escalation ...

JACKIE: Like closing a few more pits?

EXPERT: Rationalise our existing resources.

JACKIE: Like closing a few more pits?

EXPERT: Get our priorities right.

JACKIE: And how are you going to achieve all your aims?

EXPERT: By closing a few more pits ...

THOMAS: How many more ...

EXPERT: Well, in non-technical language ... most of them ...

GEORDIE: What's Alf Robens say about this?

EXPERT: Please ...

(He takes a couple of tranquillisers.)

A delightful man, really ... just ... well, my business really ... high speed gas ...

(Very troubled.)

THOMAS: A word with you.

EXPERT: Certainly, brother ...

THOMAS: We made your Movement what it is ...

EXPERT: Nobody recognises more than us the great debt the Labour movement owes to the miners . . .

THOMAS: My grandson works at Datton Colliery, and they can produce coal that's cheaper per unit than either high speed gas or high speed nuclear power or high speed anything else . . .

JACKIE: And production's gone up by 60% in the last seven years . . . that's better than any private industry can claim . . .

GEORDIE: And the Durham coalfield's running at a profit . . .

JACKIE: And there hasn't been a serious industrial dispute in twenty years . . .

THOMAS: Right?

EXPERT (checking his notebook): Right . . .

THOMAS: So you're closing all the pits?

EXPERT: Taking the broad view . . .

JACKIE: Thank you very much.

THOMAS: No, listen . . . You're not shutting them because it's a terrible job that kills men and makes widows and orphans . . .

EXPERT: We're simply taking the broad view.

WILL: You're not closing them because of the broken backs and silicosis . . .

EXPERT: We're simply re-assessing our priorities . . .

WILL: You're not closing them because you want us and our children to have a cleaner, safer, better life . . .

EXPERT: Not in so many words, it's the technological revolution . . . I mean, if you consider the National Economy as a big iced cake . . .

THOMAS: Oh, hadaway to Hell!

(Pause.)

EXPERT: I do have some good news.

JACKIE: What?

EXPERT: It's full steam ahead on the perfume factory.

(They chase him off.)

THOMAS: You'll not remember Ramsay McDonald.

WILL: I do . . . the bastard.

GEORDIE: But what's the alternative?

MARY (at window): Here's the alternative coming up the path now.

JACKIE: Ye what?

(Fanfare.)

SLIDE: 1972.

THOMAS: 1972. Edward Heath.

JACKIE: Robert Carr.

GEORDIE: John Davies.

WILL: The Comedians!

(Pause.)

THOMAS: Edward Heath.

(Two quick bars of All the Nice Girls Love a Sailor and EXPERT comes on as Sailor Ted.)

GEORDIE (to audience as Groucho): And this is where the story really starts, folks.

WILL: Have ye dropped in to explain the Government's fuel policy?

TED: Certainly not. We don't believe in policies, as such.

THOMAS: That's a relief.

TED: We believe every lame duck should stand on his good foot.

JACKIE: So what are you after?

TED: I'm looking for a mooring.

JACKIE: A mooring?

TED: A handy spot to tie up.

THOMAS: Tie what up?

TED: My great white ship.

WILL: What great white ship would that be?

(Pause.)

TED: Tell me. How many of you have heard of the North Sea?

GEORDIE: Why aye, I've had a piddle in there, I mean a paddle, no, I've said that bit . . .

JACKIE: Now had on a minute . . .

TED: And what lies *beyond* the North Sea full forty thousand leagues?

THOMAS: Beyond?

TED: Beyond.

GEORDIE: Northern Ireland is it?

TED (pained): Please . . . I am referring to no less than Europe.

WILL: Europe?

TED: And on my great white ship, myself at the helm, we shall steer through the foaming breakers into that great dawn that lies ahead, that dawn that will herald our joining hands with our European partners — Beethoven, Wagner, Mozart — in the Promised Land of Tomorrow.

MARY: Why that sounds grand.

WILL: On your great white ship?

TED: Sur mon grand bateau blanc.

JACKIE: If you're as good as you say you are why don't you just walk across.

WILL (to THOMAS): He's a right queer bugger, this one.

THOMAS: You'll not remember Stanley Baldwin.

GEORDIE: And what are we doing while you're steering?

TED: You will be the crew.

JACKIE: If we're ganna be the crew, we'll want a pay rise.

TED: You can have a pay rise.

JACKIE: How much?

TED: N minus one per cent.

GEORDIE: What's that in numbers?

TED (checks pocket book): That'll be seven per cent.

JACKIE: Twenty-five per cent.

TED: I'll consider a compromise. Say . . . seven point nine per cent.

JACKIE: Twenty-five.

TED: The nation will not be held to ransom. I, Stanley Baldwin, that's to say, Neville Chamberlain, that's to say, Edward Heath . . .

JACKIE (breaking in): I, Joe Gormley, say twenty-five per cent.

(All the lights go out. Blackout.)

TED: I, Edward, said . . . let there be light, and there was light.

(A single candle is lit on stage. Music starts.)

ALL: Strike! Strike! Strike! Strike! Strike!

(A candle is lit on each word: Strike! Then the song.)

FRANK: Strike a match and light a candle.

RUTH: Let it shine, bonny lad . . .

VICAR: Let it shine . . .

GEORDIE: But not for Jesus,

THOMAS: Let it shine for us, me lad.

ALL:
Let it shine, let it shine,
Let it shine, bonny lad,
Strike a match and light a candle
Let it shine, let it shine.

(The chorus can be repeated, as more candles are lit.)

JACKIE (speaking): You know, I'm getting a bit sick of lighting candles. I've got another idea.

(As he sings his verse, he addresses the others in turn but getting negative response from all except maybe FRANK and RUTH.)

Sings:
Strike a match and light the fuses,
Let it burn, bonny lad,
Let it burn but not for Jesus,
Let it burn for us, me lad.
Let it burn, let it burn,
Let it burn, bonny lad.
Strike a match and light the fuses,
Let it burn, let it burn.

(The music continues under as the lights go on. They look around but the EXPERT has gone.)

JACKIE: Where's he gone?

MARY: I don't know . . . but he left this out the back.

(MARY holds up a ship's lifebelt: on it is written 17%.)

WILL: What's that it says on it?

MARY: Seventeen per cent. Kind regards. Wilberforce.

JACKIE: The biggest pay rise in the history of the British Labour Movement. The strike they said we couldn't win and we won it . . .

THOMAS: Hang on a minute, Jackie lad . . . you're talking about money.

JACKIE: Why aye, I'm talking about money. I'm talking about the fruits of wer labours.

THOMAS: But it's not about money. You weren't singing about money. Like, it was still *Lord* Wilberforce that decided . . .

JACKIE: What? Is it a revolution ye want?

THOMAS: Well . . . I'm a bit too tired myself. But if I was younger . . .

(Pause.)

At least I wouldn't be scared of winning!

GEORDIE: But howay man Tommy, it couldn't happen here.

(And into the song: It Couldn't Happen Here. A chorus song with individuals singing the verses. Loud and robust and angry.)

ALL:
It couldn't happen here, no, it couldn't happen here,
We've made a little Eden so it couldn't happen here.

GEORDIE:
We need no revolution to achieve the things we've planned,

No fighting in the streets for us, we've got the promised land.

ALL:
So it couldn't happen here, no, it couldn't happen here,
No fighting in the streets for us, so it couldn't happen here.

VICAR:
There are no more injustices in this dear island home,
Equality, Fraternity and Liberty are won.

ALL:
So it couldn't happen here, no, it couldn't happen here,
There are no more injustices, so it couldn't happen here.

WILL:
There are no idle rich men now who profit from the poor,
There are no landed gentry shooting grouse upon the moor.

ALL:
So it couldn't happen here, no it couldn't happen here,
There are no landed gentry, so it couldn't happen here.

FRANK:
There is no exploitation so why should we try to change,
For no-one's making thousands playing on the Stock Exchange.

ALL:
So it couldn't happen here, no, it couldn't happen here,
For no-one's making thousands so it couldn't happen here.

JACKIE:
And even in adversity we share an equal role,
Just witness all the stockbrokers a-waiting at the dole.

ALL:
So it couldn't happen here, no, it couldn't happen here,
Just witness all the stockbrokers, so it couldn't happen here.

MARY and RUTH:
There are no wicked landlords here who charge excessive rent,
Our peasants own the land, you see, that's why they're quite content.

ALL:
So it couldn't happen here, no, it couldn't happen here,
Our peasants own the land, you see, so it couldn't happen here.

THOMAS:
There are no royal palaces with a thousand empty rooms,
There are no people forced to live in dirty stinking slums.

ALL:
So it couldn't happen here, no it couldn't happen here,
There are no royal palaces so it couldn't happen here.

(A big loud finish. Out of it emerges a knocking at the door.)

MARY: There's somebody at the door.

THOMAS: You're hearing things, woman.

MARY: I'm telling you there is . . .

(And there is. And a slow realisation of what it might mean.)

I'll go.

(MARY goes to the door. She greets HUGHIE — the pit messenger.)

HUGHIE: Mrs Milburn.

MARY: You know it is . . .

HUGHIE: Your grandson John works at the pit . . .

MARY: I know he does . . .

HUGHIE: There's been an accident.

RUTH: No . . .

THOMAS: Quiet!

MARY: What sort of accident?

HUGHIE: A fall of stone . . . John was working with his maintenance gang
. . . on the face . . . we don't know exactly where they are . . . just the
other side . . . no contact, you see . . .

(Silent reactions.)

As soon as there's any more news.

MARY: Yes.

HUGHIE: Other calls to make.

MARY: Yes.

(HUGHIE goes out. No conversation. Just quiet music playing, perhaps a
guitar or mouth-organ. Into the following sequence which is played, hard
and simply, in a very domestic context of tea-making and drinking — the
normal crisis reaction.)

There might be something on the news.

FRANK (as Radio One announcer): News is coming in of an accident at
Datton Colliery in . . . County Durham, no further details as yet. Meanwhile, Gary Sobers is piling up the runs in the final test. Weather tomorrow, continuing unsettled. Now back to Earl Bartok and his midnight
disc-a-go-go-round . . .

(Fade up loud on tape a hideous pop noise which quickly fades and out
of it emerges the quiet music link previously established. THOMAS
speaks.)

THOMAS: He walks about like a god, afraid of no-one. If he feels like
working, he works. Nobody can hold the big whip over him. It doesn't
exist. Sometimes he's got a lot of money, sometimes he's broke to the
wide. He likes to gamble with his money. Sometimes he wins; occasionally
he doesn't. Inside his particular prison he possesses liberty. My lad, dour,

hard as the rock they tunnel, contradictory and uncertain to understand unless you know the way the cleat of their nature runs. But this is the way they are made; the way they have to be.

(Music link.)

FRANK (as announcer): Latest news of the pit disaster. Eight men are trapped behind a fall of rock and rescue teams are hard at work. Two new records broken today . . . at Sotheby's for a Rubens and by Tottenham Hotspur for a left-winger . . .

(Music link.)

VICAR: Come unto me, all ye men that labour and are heavy laden, and I will give you rest.
Take my yoke unto you and learn of me; for I am meek and lowly in heart; and ye shall find rest unto your souls. For my yoke is easy and my burden is light.

JACKIE: Lucky you.

(Music link.)

FRANK (as announcer): A big surprise in today's Top Twenty. Harry Dingle, the Hammersmith milkman, shoots to number one spot with his own composition . . . 'A Penny for your Thoughts, you filthy devil' . . . meanwhile, no more news from Datton Colliery.

(Music link.)

JACKIE: He works in order to live. What he produces for himself is not the silk that he weaves, not the gold that he draws from the mines, not the palace that he builds. What he produces for himself is wages, and silk, gold, palaces resolve themselves into the means of subsistence . . . a cotton jacket, some copper coins, and a lodging . . . And the worker . . . does he consider his weaving, spinning, drilling, turning, building, shovelling, stone breaking as a manifestation of his life, as life? On the contrary, life begins for him when this activity ends . . . He does not even reckon labour as part of his life, it is rather a sacrifice of his life.

(Music link.)

FRANK (as announcer): And it's closing down time from your Radio Wonderful station, good night, everybody, and if you're still up, having a party, celebrating some great family occasion, well, have yourselves a swinging time, so good night, stay bright and it's yours truly saying 'bye for now.

(The last bars of signature tune. The first bars of National Anthem, abruptly switched off. Then a silence and a waiting. Everybody self-consciously drinking tea, trying and failing to think of anything to say. Till the pithead bell rings.)

THOMAS: Will . . . ?

WILL: I'm here, ye daft beggar . . . .

MARY: Will's here . . .

(And they realise. They all dash to the pithead and THOMAS sets the winding gear going. The cage appears and out of it step JOHN and his mates — in their pitgear, helmets, black faces.)

John . . .

JOHN: Who did you think? The bloody Black and White minstrel show?

THOMAS: What happened, lad?

JOHN: We remembered your story . . . we just kept on walking till we came to the old shaft . . . and here we are, well, ye divven like to miss a party . . .

WILL: Ye bugs.

RUTH: John.

(RUTH rushes to him. They embrace, then JOHN leads her gently by the hand and returns her to FRANK.)

JOHN: That's your man.

RUTH: Is it?

JOHN: You don't need a pitman . . . and Frank needs you . . . look after his black eyes . . .

RUTH: Does that mean you're staying in the village?

JOHN: I didn't say so. I'll maybe gan somewhere where they need big strong men.

THOMAS: It's time you cleared off . . .

JOHN: Ye what?

MARY: We don't want you hanging round wor necks all wor lives . . .

THOMAS: Gan out into the world, John lad . . . staying home like this, you're stifling our independence . . .

MARY: Anyways, the village is finished . . . dead . . .

(JACKIE and GEORDIE step forward, very casual and conversational but apart from the main group.)

JACKIE: I reckon young John wants to get hisself a job in engineering, somethin' like that . . . he's a skilled man, y'know . . .

GEORDIE: He could go to one of the big engineering works on Teesside . . .

JACKIE: What on the mighty Teesside conurbation?

GEORDIE: Why, aye, man.

JACKIE: 'Cause I reckon coalmining's very near finished . . .

GEORDIE: And about bloody time, an' all . . .

JACKIE: Anyhow, they'll sort something out . . . the other two'll gan back to Jesmond and get on with their post-graduate researches . . .

GEORDIE: Dirty beasts . . .

JACKIE: Eh?

GEORDIE: Young married couple . . . he says to her, do you fancy half an hour on the rug . . . no, she says . . . oh dear, he says, we'll never get that rug finished . . . .

JACKIE: Anyhow, it's only a story . . .

GEORDIE: Is it?

JACKIE: Actors dressed up.

GEORDIE: Getaway.

JACKIE: They'll be down the Labour Exchange like the rest of us when this job's finished . . .

GEORDIE: I never knew that . . . maybes they could march on Whitehall, stir the conscience of the nation . . .

JACKIE: Maybe they will.

GEORDIE: I'll tell you somethin', Jackie, though . . .

JACKIE: What?

GEORDIE: Ye says it's only a story . . .

JACKIE: Aye.

GEORDIE: It's a canny old story . . .

(Into the song. A chorus song, addressed to the audience. The verses hard and bitter. The choruses jolly. During the song, the stage is filled with the whole cast, the band in uniform, lodge banners, portraits of the great men: Tommy Hepburn, Martin Jude, Tommy Burt, William Crawford and Sam Watson. Till at the end the stage is full of gutsy movement and hard colour.)

ALL:
It's only a story, a story, a story,
It's only a story, a fanciful tale,
Just ask the rich pitmen who live here in Jesmond,
It's only a story, a fanciful tale.

JACKIE:
There's no need to weep and there's no need to moan
So wipe out the memories and tek yourself home.

ALL:
It's only a story, a story, a story,
It's only a story, a fanciful tale,
Just ask the rich pitmen who live here in Jesmond,
It's only a story, a fanciful tale.

GEORDIE:
And nobody suffered and nobody died
And no-one went hungry and no widows cried.

ALL:
    It's only a story, a story, a story,
    It's only a story, a fanciful tale,
    Just ask the rich pitmen who live here in Jesmond,
    It's only a story, a fanciful tale.

THOMAS:
    There were no strikes or lock-outs, no gas in the seam
    No, none of it happened, it's all a bad dream.

ALL:
    It's only a story, a story, a story,
    It's only a story, a fanciful tale,
    Just ask the rich pitmen who live here in Jesmond,
    It's only a story, a fanciful tale.

ALL:
    So off you go home to your bright cosy fire
    Throw a shovel more coal on the funeral pyre.

ALL:
    It's only a story, a story, a story,
    It's only a story, a fanciful tale,
    Just ask the rich pitmen who live here in Jesmond,
    It's only a story, a fanciful tale.

    (And the music continues, more quietly, and changing the tune, as JOHN moves forward.)

JOHN (sings, unaccompanied):
    Close the coalhouse door, lad,
    There's blood inside.
    Geordie's standing at the dole,
    And Mrs Jackson, like a fool,
    Complains about the price of coal.

    Close the coalhouse door, lad,
    There's blood inside,
    There's bones inside,
    There's bairns inside,
    So stay outside.

    (A silence, a pause, then everybody turns quickly towards the pithead. They bow their heads in brief homage. A fade to blackout.)

Song p.11

Each verse is a preface to a separate Act. That is the second verse opens the second Act and the third verse opens the third Act. The fourth verse, however, is set at the very end of the play as a coda to the final song, and is written out in full on page 78.

Song p.18

When that I was and a little tiny boy, Me daddy said to me, 'The time has come, me bonny bonny bairn, To learn your A B C.' Now Daddy was a Lodge Chairman In the coalfields of the Tyne And that A B C was different From the Enid Blyton kind. He sang:

A is for Alienation that made me the man that I am and B's for the boss who's a bastard, a bourgeois who don't give a damn.

All the alphabet couplets C/D, E/F, etc up to U/V are as above in the repeated section.

W is for all willing workers and that's where the memory fades for X Y and Z, me dear daddy said, will be written on the street barricades. And now that I'm not a

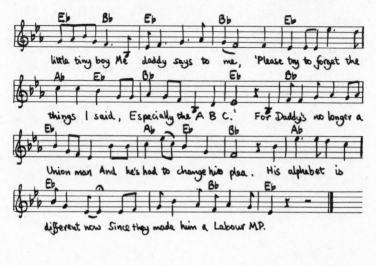

little tiny boy Me daddy says to me, 'Please try to forget the things I said, Especially the A B C.' For Daddy's no longer a Union man And he's had to change his plea. His alphabet is different now Since they made him a Labour M.P.

Song p.23

Time for to make a stand, me lads, Time for to take a hand, me lads, Time for us to unite, me lads, Time for to start a fight, me lads. Time, Time, Time, Time for to get the pitman some justice and peace —

Twenty long weeks, twenty long weeks, bonny black bird, twenty long weeks, Singin' that song, like nothin' was wrong, haven't you heard? Twenty long weeks.

Both second and third verses are accompanied by the men singing 'Time' very softly as a counterpoint.

Song p.27

Twenty long weeks,

Time for to make a stand, me lads Time for to take a twenty long weeks, canny black bird,

hand, me lads Time for us to unite, me lads, Time for to start a twenty long weeks, Yon soft feathered breast, may warm the bairn's

fight, me lads. Time, Time, Time.

nest But my bairn lies dead; Twenty long weeks.

Time for to get the pitmen some justice and peace

Song p.28

Somebody cares, somebody cares

So nice to know, lads that somebody cares.

Just pick up your supplement See how they care The

good things of life, lads They want you to share

Brand new Cortinas And Washin' machines

Stop here in verse 3 for dialogue

Wall to Wall Carpets And tins o' Bile Beans

D/C chorus

The third verse stops where indicated on the previous page. The final chorus is as follows:

Song p.30 Each clause of the Miners' Regulations Bill is punctuated by a line from 'Time'.

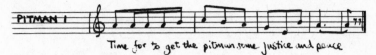

PITMAN 1

Time for to get the pitman some justice and peace

Song p.32

Let's drink to the Union, the Union, the Union, The Union that's strong as a good pint of beer. Downstairs in the bar they've got pints lined up waiting As soon as you've supped them we'll see you back here. So drink to the Union, the Union, the Union, As soon as you've supped them, we'll see you back here.

Song p.36

My old man's a Union man As happy as happy can be he spends his life on a piece-work plan But it

brings no peace to me. When he comes home at the

break of dawn He gives to me this greetin':

Mary dear, ye've nowt to fear—I've been to a Union

meetin'.

Song p.45

Not a penny off the pay Not a

minute on the day. A - men. Blessed

are the coal owners who make such fair demands.

Blessed are the blacklegs who come from foreign lands.

Blessed are the constables with truncheons in their hands

A — men And the voice of the miners was heard and the

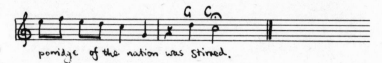

porridge of the nation was stirred.

Song p.47

I should have done it yesterday If I
hadn't had a cold But since I've put this pint away, I've
never felt so bold. So as soon as this pub closes, As
soon as this pub closes, As soon as this pub closes, The
revolution starts.

Song p.52

When me father was a lad unem-
ploy ment was so bad He spent best part of his
life down at the dole. Straight from

e mi

school to the labour queue Raggy clothes and holey

G   D   G

shoes Combin' pit-heaps for a manky bag o' coal.

D   C

And I'm standin' at the door, at the

D   C

same old bloody door, Waiting for the

D   C

pay-out as me father did be-fore

Song p.56

C   F

When it's ours, Geordie lad, when it's

C   G (spoken)

ours, There'll be changes, bonny lad, when it's ours. When

C   C⁷   F   D⁷

us colliers take control, No more twelve-inch seams of coal, No more

C   G   C F C

means-test, no more dole, When it's ours, all ours.

Song p.64

(spoken) F   ðmi

If you ever go to Tyneside you must

Bb   C   d mi   G

watch your P's and Q's, You must learn to say Newcassel or their

G⁷   C   A⁷   d mi

confidence you'll lose. And in mingling with the common folk

B⁷   ðmi   C   d mi

you're sure to make a botch If you ask for pints of bitter, What you

G⁷   C   F

really want is Scotch. But there's one thing makes the

d mi   Bb   C F

locals really fall into your lap Get your picture in the

       C F   Bb

papers with a little cloth cap; A little cloth

F   Bb F

cap, a little cloth cap, You'll make a big im-

       C F

pression with a little cloth cap.

Song p.73

Strike a match and light the fu-ses,
Let it burn, bon-ny lad, Let it burn but
not for Jesus Let it burn for us, me lad.
Let it burn, let it burn, Let it burn,
bonny lad Strike a match and light the fuses
Let it burn, let it burn.

Song p.73

It couldn't happen here, no, it couldn't happen here, We've made a little Eden so it couldn't happen here, We need no revo-lution to achieve the things we've planned, No fighting in the streets for us we've got the promised land, So it

Song p.74

FINAL CHORUS AS FOLLOWS:

So it couldn't happen here, no it couldn't happen here, there are no royal palaces so it couldn't happen here.

Song p.78

It's only a story, a story, a story, It's only a story, a fanciful tale, Just ask the rich pitmen that live here in Jesmond, It's only a story, a fanciful tale. There's no need to weep and there's no need to moan So wipe out the memories and tek yourself home. It's

At the end of the final chorus, modulate to C sharp minor for the fourth verse of 'Close the Coalhouse Door'.

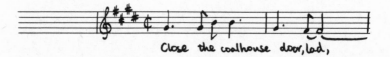

Close the coalhouse door, lad,